G000254403

MISCHIEF FESTIVAL

MISCHIEF FESTIVAL

THE EARTHWORKS
by Tom Morton-Smith

MYTH
by Matt Hartley and Kirsty Housley
From an original idea by Kirsty Housley

OBERON BOOKS
LONDON

WWW.OBERONBOOKS.COM

First published in 2017 by Oberon Books Ltd
521 Caledonian Road, London N7 9RH
Tel: +44 (0) 20 7607 3637 / Fax: +44 (0) 20 7607 3629
e-mail: info@oberonbooks.com
www.oberonbooks.com

PB ISBN: 978-1-78682-217-8
E ISBN: 978-1-78682-218-5

Printed, bound and converted
by CPI Group (UK) Ltd, Croydon, CR0 4YY.

Visit www.oberonbooks.com to read more about all our books and to buy
them. You will also find features, author interviews and news of any author
events, and you can sign up for e-newsletters so that you're always first to
hear about our new releases.

Contents

ABOUT THE ROYAL SHAKESPEARE COMPANY

The Shakespeare Memorial Theatre opened in Stratford-upon-Avon in 1879. Since then the plays of Shakespeare have been performed here, alongside the work of his contemporaries and of living modern playwrights. In 1960, the Royal Shakespeare Company was formed, gaining its Royal Charter in 1961. The founding principles of the Company were threefold: the Company would embrace the freedom and power of Shakespeare's work, train and develop young actors and directors and, crucially, experiment in new ways of making theatre. The RSC quickly became known for exhilarating performances of Shakespeare alongside new masterpieces such as *The Homecoming* and *Old Times* by Harold Pinter. It was a combination that thrilled audiences and this close and exacting relationship between writers from different eras has become the fuel that powers the creativity of the RSC.

In 1974, The Other Place opened in a tin hut on Waterside under the visionary leadership and artistic directorship of Buzz Goodbody. Determined to explore Shakespeare's plays in intimate proximity to her audience and to make small-scale, radical new work, Buzz revitalised the Company's interrogation between the contemporary and classical repertoire. Reopened in 2016 under the artistic directorship of Erica Whyman, The Other Place is once again the home for experimentation and the development of exciting new ideas.

In our 55 years of producing new plays, we have collaborated with some of the most exciting writers of their generation. These have included: Edward Albee, Howard Barker, Alice Birch, Richard Bean, Edward Bond, Howard Brenton, Marina Carr, Caryl Churchill, Martin Crimp, David Edgar, Helen Edmundson, James Fenton, Georgia Fitch, Fraser Grace, David Greig, Tanika Gupta, Matt Hartley, Ella Hickson, Kirsty Housley, Dennis Kelly, Anders Lustgarten, Tarell Alvin McCraney, Martin McDonagh, Tom Morton-Smith, Rona Munro, Richard Nelson, Anthony Neilson, Harold Pinter, Phil Porter, Mike Poulton, Mark Ravenhill, Somalia Seaton, Adriano Shaplin, Tom Stoppard, debbie tucker green, Frances Ya-Chu Cowhig, Timberlake Wertenbaker, Peter Whelan and Roy Williams.

The Company today is led by Gregory Doran, whose appointment as Artistic Director represents a long-term commitment to the disciplines and craftsmanship required to put on the plays of Shakespeare. The RSC under his leadership is committed to illuminating the relevance of Shakespeare's plays and the works of his contemporaries for the next generation of audiences and believes that our continued investment in new plays and living writers is an essential part of that mission.

The RSC is grateful for the significant support of its principal funder, Arts Council England, without which our work would not be possible. Around 75 per cent of the RSC's income is self-generated from Box Office sales, sponsorship, donations, enterprise and partnerships with other organisations.

Supported using public funding by
ARTS COUNCIL ENGLAND

NEW WORK AT THE RSC

We are a contemporary theatre company built on classical rigour. Through an extensive programme of research and development, we resource writers, directors and actors to explore and develop new ideas for our stages, and as part of this we commission playwrights to engage with the muscularity and ambition of the classics and to set Shakespeare's world in the context of our own.

We invite writers to spend time with us in our rehearsal rooms, with our actors and creative teams. Alongside developing new plays for all our stages, we invite playwrights to contribute dramaturgically to both our productions of Shakespeare and his contemporaries, as well as our work for, and with, young people. We believe that engaging with living writers and contemporary theatre-makers helps to establish a creative culture within the Company which both inspires new work and creates an ever more urgent sense of enquiry into the classics.

Shakespeare was a great innovator and breaker of rules, as well as a bold commentator on the times in which he lived. It is his spirit which informs new work at the RSC. Erica Whyman, Deputy Artistic Director, heads up this strand of the Company's work alongside Pippa Hill as Literary Manager.

The work of the RSC Literary Department is generously supported by
THE DRUE HEINZ TRUST.

The spring 2017 *Mischief Festival* was first presented by the Royal Shakespeare Company in The Other Place, Stratford-upon-Avon, on 24 May 2017. The cast was as follows:

The Earthworks by Tom Morton-Smith

HERTA	**REBECCA HUMPHRIES**
CLARE	**LENA KAUR**
FRITJOF	**THOMAS MAGNUSSEN**

Myth by Matt Hartley and Kirsty Housley, from an original idea by Kirsty Housley

GEORGE	**FEHINTI BALOGUN**
SARAH	**REBECCA HUMPHRIES**
LAURA	**LENA KAUR**
TOM	**THOMAS MAGNUSSEN**

The RSC Acting Companies are generously supported by THE GATSBY CHARITABLE FOUNDATION and THE KOVNER FOUNDATION.

The Earthworks

Director	**Erica Whyman**
Designer	**Rosanna Vize**
Lighting Designer	**Mark Tolan**
Composer	**Sarah Llewellyn**
Sound Designer	**Steven Atkinson**
Voice Work	**Anna McSweeney**
Assistant Director	**Zoé Ford**
Casting Director	**Annelie Powell**
Dramaturg	**Pippa Hill**
Production Manager	**Julian Cree**
Costume Supervisor	**Zarah Meherali**
Company Stage Manager	**Julia Wade**
Assistant Stage Managers	**Ruth Blakey**
	PK Thummukgool
Producer	**Claire Birch**

Myth

Director	**Kirsty Housley**
Designer	**Rosanna Vize**
Lighting Designer	**Jonathan Laidlow**
Composer	**Sarah Llewellyn**
Sound Designer	**Steven Atkinson**
Movement Director	**Naomi Said**
Voice Work	**Anna McSweeney**
Assistant Director	**Sophie Moniram**
Associate Movement Director	**Jonnie Riordan**
Casting Director	**Annelie Powell**
Dramaturg	**Nic Wass**
Production Manager	**Julian Cree**
Costume Supervisor	**Zarah Meherali**
Company Stage Manager	**Julia Wade**
Assistant Stage Managers	**Ruth Blakey**
	PK Thummukgool
Producer	**Claire Birch**

This text may differ slightly from the play as performed.

The contribution of Sarah Llewellyn to this production was made possible through the Cameron Mackintosh Resident Composer Scheme, managed by Mercury Musical Developments and Musical Theatre Network and supported by the Mackintosh Foundation.

LOVE THE RSC?

Become a Member or Patron and support our work

The RSC is a registered charity. Our aim is to stage theatre at its best, made in Stratford-upon-Avon and shared around the world with the widest possible audience and we need your support.

Become an RSC Member from £50 per year and access up to three weeks of Priority Booking, advance information, exclusive discounts and special offers, including free on-the-day seat upgrades.

Or support as a Patron from £150 per year for up to one additional week of Priority Booking, plus enjoy opportunities to discover more through special behind-the-scenes events.

For more information visit **www.rsc.org.uk/support** or call the RSC Membership Office on 01789 403440.

THE ROYAL SHAKESPEARE COMPANY

CAST

FEHINTI BALOGUN
GEORGE
RSC DEBUT SEASON: *Myth*.
TRAINED: RADA.
THEATRE: *King Lear* (Old Vic).
THEATRE WHILST TRAINING:
Agamemnon, Coriolanus, The Country Wife, All's Well That Ends Well, Dying for It, In Arabia We'd All Be Kings.

REBECCA HUMPHRIES
HERTA/SARAH
RSC DEBUT SEASON: *The Earthworks, Myth*.
THEATRE INCLUDES: *Wild Honey, The Argument* (Hampstead Theatre); *Pomona* (National Theatre/Orange Tree/Royal Exchange); *Temple* (Donmar Warehouse); *Open Court: Primetime* (Royal Court); *The Kitchen* (National Theatre); *24 Hour Plays* (Old Vic).
TELEVISION INCLUDES: *The Agency, Cockroaches, Big Bad World, Come Fly With Me, Cardinal Burns*.

LENA KAUR
CLARE/LAURA
RSC: *The Two Noble Kinsmen, The Rover, The Seven Acts of Mercy*.
THIS SEASON: *The Earthworks, Myth*.
THEATRE INCLUDES: *Around the World in 80 Days* (St James Theatre); *The Ghost Train* (Manchester Royal Exchange); *Treasure Island* (National Theatre); *Thursday* (ETT/Australian tour); *Are You That Girl off the Telly?* (Hen and Chickens); *Sisters* (Sheffield Theatres); *Rubina* (Birmingham Rep); *The Sky's the Limit* (Old Vic); *Free World* (Contact); *Silent Cry* (West Yorkshire Playhouse).
TELEVISION INCLUDES: *Happy Valley, Stargazing, Justin's House, Dead Cert, Doctors, Dani's Castle, Prisoners' Wives, Torchwood, Emmerdale, Speechless, Hollyoaks, Scallywagga, Torn*.
FILM: *The Endz*.
RADIO INCLUDES: *Reality Check, Silver Street, Maps for Lost Lovers*.

THOMAS MAGNUSSEN
FRITJOF/TOM
RSC DEBUT SEASON: *The Earthworks*, *Myth*.
THEATRE INCLUDES: *Testamentet: The Testament, Hamlet, Thor* (Royal Danish Theatre); *Arabian Nights* (Zeppelin Theatre); *Long Day's Journey Into Night* (Folketeatret. dk); *Flugten* (NyAveny); *Twelfth Night* (Republique); *Muse of Fire* (Kaleidoskop. Winner, with Lars Mikkelsen, of the prestigious Aarets Reumert stage award); *Heroes Inc* (That Theatre Co); *Jesus & Josefine* (Odense Teater); *The Little Foxes* (Det Danske Teater); *The Awakening of Spring* (Mungo Park); *Lord of the Flies* (Odsherred Teater).
TELEVISION INCLUDES: *Band of Brothers, The Bridge, The Inheritance, Follow the Money*.
FILM INCLUDES: *Secluded, Hush Little Baby, Aurum, Two Brothers*.

CREATIVE TEAM

STEVEN ATKINSON
SOUND DESIGNER
RSC: *Fall of the Kingdom, Rise of the Foot Soldier; Always Orange; King Lear* (Barbican re-design), *Cymbeline* (Barbican re-design). Steven is currently a member of the RSC Sound Department. THIS SEASON: *The Earthworks*, *Myth*. TRAINED: University of Huddersfield, BA (Hons) Music Production.
WORK INCLUDES: Following training, Steven worked for several years in his native St. Albans as both a theatre technician and later as venue manager. In 2011 he joined the RSC Sound Department for the inaugural season in the redeveloped theatres. Since then he has toured for the RSC numerous times as Senior Sound Technician, and has taken shows across the UK and installed residencies for RSC productions in Newcastle, the Roundhouse and the Barbican. In 2016, Steven took the *King & Country* season of shows to mainland China, the Hong Kong Arts Festival and the Brooklyn Academy of Music.

ZOÉ FORD
ASSISTANT DIRECTOR
RSC DEBUT SEASON: *Antony and Cleopatra, The Earthworks*.
Zoé was Artistic Director of independent theatrical production company Hiraeth Artistic Productions from 2011-2014. Following this she held the Resident Assistant Director position at the Donmar Warehouse and, previous to this, was Text Assistant at Shakespeare's Globe.
THEATRE INCLUDES: For Hiraeth Artistic Productions: *Hamlet* (Riverside Studios. Off West End nomination for Best Director); *Richard III, Romeo and Juliet, A Life in the Theatre* (Gatehouse); *Titus Andronicus* (Arcola/Edinburgh Fringe/Etcetera); *Blood Wedding* (Waterloo East). Other theatre includes: *Macbeth* (Mountview Academy of Arts); *Sonnets* (Shakespeare's Globe); *Click 2 Share* (Theatre503); *Wounds* (Tristan Bates); *The School for Scandal* (Waterloo East).

As the Donmar Warehouse Resident Assistant Director: *Les Liaisons Dangereuses*, *Closer*, *Teddy Ferrara*, *Vote*, *Splendour*, as well as directing and editing the Donmar Warehouse cast recording of *Les Liaisons Dangereuses* by Choderlos de Laclos (Donmar Warehouse/Audible/Wireless Theatre Co). Other assisting credits include: *Henry V* (Regent's Park Open Air Theatre). As Text Assistant at Shakespeare's Globe: *The Comedy of Errors*, *Hamlet*, *Titus Andronicus*, *Julius Caesar*.

MATT HARTLEY
PLAYWRIGHT
RSC DEBUT SEASON: *Myth*.
TRAINED: Drama at the University of Hull.
THEATRE INCLUDES: Matt's first play, *Sixty Five Miles*, won a Bruntwood Award in the inaugural Bruntwood Competition and was produced by Paines Plough/Hull Truck. Other work includes: *Here I Belong* (Pentabus); *Deposit* (Hampstead Theatre); *Horizon* (National Theatre Connections); *Microcosm* (Soho Theatre); *The Bee* (Edinburgh Festival); *Punch* (Hampstead Theatre/Heat and Light Co); *Epic*, *Trolls*, *Life for Beginners* (Theatre503). Matt's play *Deposit* is currently being revived by the Hampstead Theatre and *Here I Belong* will be re-mounted by Pentabus in spring 2018. Matt's work is regularly performed in Europe and his play *Burning Cars* will receive its world premiere in Paris in 2018. Matt is currently writing new plays for Hampstead Theatre and West Yorkshire Playhouse.
RADIO INCLUDES: *The Pursuit*, *Final Call* (Radio 4).

PIPPA HILL
DRAMATURG
RSC: *The Hypocrite*, *The Seven Acts of Mercy*, *Fall of the Kingdom*, *Rise of the Foot Soldier*, *Always Orange*, *Don Quixote*, *Queen Anne*, *Hecuba*, *Oppenheimer*, *The Christmas Truce*, *The Roaring Girl*, *The Ant and the Cicada*, *I Can Hear You*, *Wendy & Peter Pan*, *The Empress*, *The Thirteen Midnight Challenges of Angelus Diablo*, *Here Lies Mary Spindler*.

THIS SEASON: *The Earthworks*.
Pippa Hill is the Literary Manager at the RSC and oversees the commissioning and development of all the Company's new plays, adaptations and translations. She also works closely with the creative teams preparing the texts for the classical repertoire. She was previously the Literary Manager at Paines Plough, running three nationwide writing initiatives designed to identify and develop new playwrights.

KIRSTY HOUSLEY
PLAYWRIGHT & DIRECTOR
RSC DEBUT SEASON: *Myth*.
THEATRE INCLUDES: *The Believers are but Brothers* (Ovalhouse/West Yorkshire Playhouse Transform17 season. Co-Director); *The Encounter* (Complicite/EIF/Warwick Arts Centre/Theatre Vidy/Bristol Old Vic. Co-Director); *Wanted* (Chris Goode and Company/Transform Festival/West Yorkshire Playhouse); *Walking the Tightrope* (Offstage/Theatre Uncut); *All I Want* (Live Theatre/Leeds Libraries/Jackson's Lane); *Mass* (Amy Mason at Bristol Old Vic/CPT); *The Beauty Project*, *Theatre Uncut 2012* (Young Vic); *How to be Immortal* (Penny Dreadful at Soho Theatre/tour); *Bandages* (Newbury Corn Exchange/tour); *9* (West Yorkshire Playhouse/Chris Goode and Company); *Thirsty* (The Paper Birds). Kirsty has been the recipient of the Oxford Samuel Beckett Theatre Trust award and the Title Pending award for innovation at Northern Stage. She is currently collaborating with Bryony Kimmings, Complicite, the Unicorn, and Bush Theatre, and is an Associate of Complicite.

JONATHAN LAIDLOW
LIGHTING DESIGNER
RSC: Jonathan joined the Lighting Department in 2016, working mainly on the Swan Season.
THIS SEASON: *Myth*.
TRAINED: Theatre Studies and Technical Stage Production at Staffordshire University.
THEATRE INCLUDES: After graduating, Jonathan worked in the lighting departments

for the West Yorkshire Playhouse and Glasgow Citizens, developing his experience programming the lighting on a variety of shows and designing the lighting for small-scale studio projects.

SARAH LLEWELLYN
COMPOSER
RSC DEBUT SEASON: RSC Composer in Residence. *The Earthworks*, *Myth*.
TRAINED: The GSMD Conservatoire.
Sarah is the founder of Tonal Music Company.
THEATRE INCLUDES: *A Tale of Two Cities* (Red Shift/Chung Ying Theatre, Hong Kong/Pleasance Edinburgh); *Natural Perspective's Britannicus* (Wilton's Music Hall/Fairbanks Shakespeare Theatre Alaska); *Antony and Cleopatra*, *Much Ado About Nothing*, *Henry V*, *The Bells*, *Caligari* (Liverpool Unity); *The Pool of Blood* (Edinburgh Fringe); *Who Will Carry the Word* (Courtyard, London); *Airswimming* (Arcola, Istanbul); *Weapons of Happiness* (Finborough Theatre); *King Arthur* (Arcola); *The Fall of Man*, *Much Ado About Nothing* (Red Shift/UK tours/Edinburgh Fringe); *Wall Talks* (Liverpool Heritage); *Misery* (Brindley Runcorn).
CIRCUS INCLUDES: With Giffords Circus: *War and Peace*, *The Saturday Book*, *Yasmine a Musical*, *Caravan*.
FILM INCLUDES: *A Short Epic About Love*, *Oscar and Jim*, *Contempt of Conscience*, *Reach Another Foundation charity*.
OTHER: At Liverpool John Moores University: *800 Years of Liverpool History*, *L8R*, *Hope and Glory*, *The Thoughtful Dresser*, *The Limehouse Golem*, *The Liver Pool of Blood*, *Oh! What a Lovely War*. Sarah recently released her own album, *10*.

ANNA McSWEENEY
VOICE WORK
RSC: Anna is a member of the Voice, Text and Actors' Support department.
THIS SEASON: *The Earthworks*, *Myth*.
Anna is a voice practitioner with an MA in Voice Studies from the Central School of Speech and Drama. She also has a BA in Acting from Guildhall School of Music and

Drama and a BA in English Literature from Warwick University. Prior to starting her role at the RSC, Anna has worked as a voice coach at a variety of London drama schools including Drama Centre, Mountview and Italia Conti.

SOPHIE MONIRAM
ASSISTANT DIRECTOR
RSC DEBUT SEASON: *Myth*.
TRAINED: Theatre Directing MA at Mountview Academy and the National Theatre Studio's Directing course.
THEATRE INCLUDES: As Director: *The Diary of a Hounslow Girl* (initially commissioned by Ovalhouse/Black Theatre Live national tour/House Theatre national tour); *POT* (Ovalhouse/Stratford Circus); *The Five Stages of Waiting* (Tristan Bates); *F**king Outside the Box* (VAULT Festival); *Indian Summer* (White Bear); *Creditors* (Cockpit Theatre); *The Star-Spangled Girl*, *Purgatorio* (Karamel Club). Sophie has also directed staged readings at Soho Theatre, Old Red Lion and the National Theatre Studio. She was the Jerwood Assistant Director on *Yerma* by Simon Stone after Lorca (Young Vic), and has also worked as Assistant Director on *Creditors* directed by Rikki Henry (Young Vic) and *The Rise and Shine of Comrade Fiasco* directed by Elayce Ismail (Gate).

TOM MORTON-SMITH
PLAYWRIGHT
RSC: *Oppenheimer* (Stratford/West End).
THIS SEASON: *The Earthworks*.
PLAYS INCLUDE: *In Doggerland* (Box of Tricks/UK tour); *Everyday Maps for Everyday Use* (Finborough Theatre/PapaTango); *Uncertainty* (Latitude Festival); *Salt Meets Wound* (Theatre503). Tom was writer-in-residence at Paines Plough Theatre Company, 2007-2008.
WORK FOR RADIO INCLUDES: *Flesh* (BBC).

JONNIE RIORDAN
ASSOCIATE MOVEMENT DIRECTOR
RSC DEBUT SEASON: *Myth*.
THEATRE INCLUDES: As Movement Director: *Maggie & Pierre* (Finborough Theatre); *Mobile*

(The Paper Birds); *Home* (Frozen Light); *Caught* (Pleasance Theatre); *A Tale of Two Cities* (USF Brit Project US); *Cracking*, *Bat Boy* (New Wimbledon Studio). As Director: *Man Up* (Frantic Assembly/Ignition); *Boy Magnet*, *White Noise* (ThickSkin). As Associate Director: *Things I Know to be True* (Frantic Assembly); *Chalk Farm*, *The Static* (ThickSkin). As a performer: *Full Stop* (Light the Fuse/Lyric Hammersmith); *Canticles* (Brighton Festival); *Overture* (Laurence Oliver Awards); *The Marriage of Figaro* (Opera Holland Park); *In His Image* (Hampstead Theatre). Jonnie is a Creative Practitioner for Frantic Assembly, delivering workshops and residencies in the UK and internationally. He is a proud graduate of Frantic's Ignition programme. He has performed for the company in productions including *This Will All Be Gone*, *No Way Back*, and for Underworld's Surreal Carnival Experiment (Alexandra Palace).

NAOMI SAID
MOVEMENT DIRECTOR
RSC: *The Taming of the Shrew*. Naomi was Resident Company Movement Practitioner at the RSC (2011-12), where projects included *The Heart of Robin Hood*, *The Comedy of Errors* and a workshop for *Much Ado About Nothing*.
THIS SEASON: *Myth*.
THEATRE INCLUDES: Movement Direction and Choreography: *Forty Years On* (Chichester); *Limehouse*, *Committee* (Donmar Warehouse); *To Kill a Mockingbird* (Regent's Park Open Air Theatre); *Whisper House* (Other Palace); *Watership Down* (Watermill); *Kevin Spacey Gala* (Old Vic); *Robin Hood* (the egg, Bath); *Scouse* (Grand Central, Liverpool); *Wasted* (West Yorkshire Playhouse). As Associate Director: *Little Dogs* (National Theatre Wales/Frantic Assembly). As Movement Associate or Assistant: *War Correspondents* (Helen Chadwick/Birmingham Rep/GDIF); *The Marriage of Figaro* (Opera Holland Park); *Lord of the Flies* (Regent's Park Open Air Theatre). Naomi has been practitioner for Frantic Assembly since 2010, facilitating educational and training workshops and

devised projects across the UK and internationally, including as Co-Director, *60 Hugs* (Ignition, Corby Cube) and Movement Consultant on *Tanika's Journey* (Deafinitely Theatre/Southwark Playhouse). As an actress: *The Curious Incident of the Dog in the Night-Time* (National Theatre/West End); *Dr Dee* (ENO/MIF). Naomi is visiting tutor at Oxford School of Drama, Royal Academy of Music, Mountview, Central and on the NT Studio Director's Course.

MARK TOLAN
LIGHTING DESIGNER
RSC: Mark is a member of the Lighting Department.
THIS SEASON: *The Earthworks*.
TRAINED: Film and Television Production at University of Westminster.
THEATRE INCLUDES: After graduating, Mark moved into technical theatre at Newcastle upon Tyne's Live Theatre. Lighting designs include: *Indiana Jones and the Extra Chair*, *Mindy* (Live Studio Theatre, Newcastle); *Carrie's War*, *Mansfield Park*, *David Copperfield* (Crucible Studio Theatre, Sheffield).

ROSANNA VIZE
DESIGNER
RSC: *A Midsummer Night's Dream* (RSC/Garsington Opera). Rosanna was Resident Design Assistant at the RSC from September 2014 to September 2015.
THIS SEASON: *The Earthworks*, *Myth*.
TRAINED: Bristol Old Vic Theatre School. Rosanna has worked regularly as an assistant to Anna Fleischle. She was a Linbury Prize Finalist in 2013, working with English Touring Opera, and is currently one of the Jerwood Young Designers.
THEATRE INCLUDES: *Low Level Panic* (Orange Tree); *After October* (Finborough Theatre); *Henry I* (Reading Between the Lines); *Girls* (Soho Theatre/HighTide/Talawa); *FUP*, *Noye's Fludde* (Kneehigh); *Dark Land Lighthouse*, *St Joan of the Stockyards*, *A Thousand Seasons Passed*, *The Tinder Box*, *The Last Days of Mankind*, *Talon* (Bristol Old

Vic); *Diary of a Madman*, *The Rise and Shine of Comrade Fiasco* (Gate); *Infinite Lives, Coastal Defences* (Tobacco Factory); *Banksy: The Room in the Elephant* (Tobacco Factory/Traverse); *Edward Gant's Amazing Feats of Loneliness*, *The Wicked Lady* (Bristol Old Vic Theatre School); *The Picture of John Grey* (Old Red Lion); *Measure for Measure* (Oxford School of Drama).
OPERA: *Don Giovanni* (Hampstead Garden Opera).

NIC WASS
DRAMATURG
RSC: Nic is Associate Dramaturg (New Work) at the RSC.
THIS SEASON: *Myth*.
THEATRE INCLUDES: Previously, Nic was Artistic Associate at the Tricycle Theatre, Deputy for the Royal Court's Literary Department and Literary Manager at Out of Joint. She has read for awards including the Bruntwood, Deafinitely Theatre, New York Summer Play Festival, Verity Bargate and George Devine Awards, as well as companies including Playful Productions, Bush Theatre, Soho Writers' Centre and Theatre503. Nic has worked with international writers from India, South Korea, Poland, Uganda and the Czech Republic, circus artists and has mentored writers within the criminal justice system. Nic was awarded the inaugural Rupert Rhymes Bursary. For the Tricycle: *The Great Wave Off Kanagawa* (Catherine Johnson Award for Best Play), *The Invisible Hand*, *The House That Will Not Stand*, *Handbagged* (Olivier Award for Outstanding Achievement in an Affiliate Theatre), *Multitudes*, *Come In! Sit Down!*, *Circles* (Catherine Johnson Award for Best Play), *The Kilburn Passion*, *The Epic Adventure of Nhamo the Manyika Warrior and his Sexy Wife Chipo* (Alfred Fagon Award shortlist); *Red Velvet* (Critics' Circle Award, Evening Standard Award). Other theatre includes: *Jinny* (Derby Theatre); *A Time to Reap*, *Vera Vera Vera* (Royal Court); *Madiya*, *Dream Story* (Gate); *The Big Fellah*, *Anderson's English* (Out of Joint/UK tour); *Faith, Hope & Charity* (Southwark Playhouse); *5,6,7,8* (Rough Cuts/Royal Court); *Ogres* (Ignition/Tristan Bates).

ERICA WHYMAN
DIRECTOR
RSC: Erica joined the RSC as Deputy Artistic Director in January 2013. As part of the Midsummer Mischief festival in 2014, Erica directed *The Ant and the Cicada, Revolt. She said. Revolt again*, soon followed by *The Christmas Truce* in the RST. In 2015 she directed *Hecuba* and in 2016 *A Midsummer Night's Dream: A Play for the Nation*, followed by the revival of *Revolt. She said. Revolt again*. for the Making Mischief festival, and *The Seven Acts of Mercy* in the Swan Theatre.
THIS SEASON: *The Earthworks*.
TRAINED: Bristol Old Vic Theatre School who awarded her an Honorary Doctorate in 2015. Erica was Chief Executive of Northern Stage in Newcastle upon Tyne from 2005 to 2012. Under her stewardship Northern Stage became known for ambitious international partnerships, the development of experimental new work especially by young theatre makers and for bold interpretations of modern classics. In 2012 she won the TMA award for Theatre Manager of the Year. Erica was Artistic Director of Southwark Playhouse (1998-2000) and then Artistic Director of the Gate Theatre, Notting Hill (2000-2004) and is a theatre director with many years' experience all over the UK.
For Northern Stage: *Son of Man*, *Ruby Moon*, *Our Friends in the North*, *A Christmas Carol*, *A Doll's House*, *Look Back in Anger*, *Hansel and Gretel*, *Oh What a Lovely War* (nominated for two TMA awards), *The Wind in the Willows*, *Who's Afraid of Virginia Woolf?* (nominated for Best Director at the 2011 TMA Awards), *The Borrowers* and the UK premiere of *Oh, the Humanity* (Edinburgh/Soho Theatre). Other work includes: *The Birthday Party* (Sheffield Crucible); *The Shadow of a Boy* (National Theatre); *The Flu Season*, *Marieluise, Witness*, *Les Justes* (Gate); *The Winter's Tale*, *The Glass Slipper* (Southwark Playhouse). In November 2016, Erica was the recipient of the Peter Brook Special Achievement Award.

This powerful double bill of plays is the result of long-term research and development at the RSC. Kirsty Housley suggested an idea, which was to become *Myth*, in response to my provocation **'What is unsayable in the 21st century?'** It was hugely ambitious; we rapidly paired Kirsty with the playwright Matt Hartley and the two of them have collaborated with a tremendous combination of invention, wit and seriousness of purpose. We were able to support periods of research with actors and then with the technical aspects of the production, so the emergence of the words as you see them here has been wholly integrated into a creation process in a rehearsal room. The thrilling theatrical experience they have imagined feels absolutely in the spirit of 'Radical Mischief' which underpins The Other Place.

It is joined by Tom Morton-Smith's beautifully surprising *The Earthworks*, which masquerades as a simple play but reaches deep into the human heart. It is a perfect answer to Tom's hugely successful and epic *Oppenheimer*, developed and produced by the RSC in 2014, as *The Earthworks* also deals with scientific brilliance, but in doing so rescues hope and wisdom from the jaws of grief and cynicism.

Both plays feel urgent and affecting; our public discourse is notably divided and the need to think, speak and act with care seems ever more urgent.

Erica Whyman, Deputy Artistic Director, May 2017

THE EARTHWORKS

For my grandfather.

With thanks to Erica Whyman, Pippa Hill,
and everyone at the RSC for their continued support.

Thanks also to Professor David Wark, John Terry,
Mel Hillyard, Nicola Samer and Jen Tan.

Characters

FRITJOF

CLARE

HERTA

The location is a hotel in Geneva.

1.

A peculiar light, natural but in the wrong place – like twilight at lunchtime.

The light comes from a rectangle of glass. At a distance this could be confused for a tablet/iPad, but it has no edges.

The light shines from a single side of the glass. The dark side isn't so much black as an absence of light – like an imploded star.

A man turns the glass in his hands. It is precious. It is the world. If he dropped it he would lose everything, but if he wrapped it in bubblewrap and locked it away it would kill the very essence of what it is.

So he holds it – carefully.

This man is called FRITJOF.

Someone is coming. FRITJOF tidies the rectangle of glass away before it is seen.

2.

Bar.

CLARE: Can I get you a drink? Can I get you a …?

FRITJOF: I was going to finish this one and then …

CLARE: … head back to your room?

FRITJOF: *(Draws attention to his wedding ring.)*

CLARE: I'm not seducing you. Oh god … no … I wasn't …
I mean … I'm sure you're very attractive, but … I am too.
Married.

FRITJOF: It's fine.

CLARE: I'm going to order a bottle of wine. I'll get two glasses.
God, it does sound like I'm cracking on to you. Red or white? Would that make a difference? Something local …
something … what's local? Do the Swiss do wine?

FRITJOF: They do fondue.

CLARE: Doesn't quite scratch the same itch, does it? Jesus, the prices in this place.

FRITJOF: Have a good evening.

CLARE: Is your wife not with you? Again, not seducing ... just small talk. Stay for another drink ... stay for five minutes. I can't sleep ... I can't ... my brain is overflowing. If I order a bottle, I'll drink a bottle ... so help a girl out?

FRITJOF: Sure.

CLARE: Is it past midnight?

FRITJOF: Yes.

CLARE: Oh, for fuck's sake. Sorry ... I've forgotten your name.

FRITJOF: I didn't give you my ...

CLARE: I'm just really bad with names.

FRITJOF: I haven't given you my name.

CLARE: No?

FRITJOF: No.

CLARE: Can I ask what it is?

FRITJOF: You can ask.

CLARE: *(Makes gesture that he should.)*

FRITJOF: Fritjof.

CLARE: Excuse me?

FRITJOF: Fritjof.

CLARE: How are you saying that?

FRITJOF: You say it ... Fritjof.

CLARE: How are you spelling that?

FRITJOF: F ... R ... I ... T ... Frit ... Jof ... J ... O ... F. Fritjof.

CLARE: And that's ... Scandi-something ... Scandiwegian?

FRITJOF: Swedish.

CLARE: Is that a common name?

FRITJOF: *(Shrugs.)*

CLARE: Sorry ... sorry ... it's awful, isn't it? I'm being very English.

FRITJOF: Don't sweat it.

CLARE: I'm sure you'd have problems with my name. I've often found people have difficulty with ...

FRITJOF: What's your name?

CLARE: Clare. But I don't spell it with an 'i', which some people find confusing.

FRITJOF: It is a pleasure to meet you, Clare.

CLARE: I can put this on expenses. I'll put this on expenses.

FRITJOF: What business are you in?

CLARE: I'm a journalist.

FRITJOF: Good night.

CLARE: Wait ... what? Don't go!

FRITJOF: Talking to journalists makes me hate the world.

CLARE: I'm nice!

FRITJOF: I'm sure that you think so.

CLARE: Has it got that bad? *(Beat.)* Look ... wine ... free wine ... a glass ... that's it. No tricks ... no con. Where else have you got to be?

FRITJOF: *(Acquiesces.)*

CLARE: Do we really get such a bad rap?

FRITJOF: Estate agents ... politicians ... journalists.

CLARE: And scientists?

FRITJOF: It depends on who you talk to.

CLARE: Are you a scientist?

FRITJOF: I am.

CLARE: I thought perhaps you didn't look like one.

FRITJOF: Um ... thanks, I guess.

CLARE: Where is everyone?

FRITJOF: It's a school night.

CLARE: Are you here for the throwing of the switch?

FRITJOF: Yes.

CLARE: The Large Hadron Collider.

FRITJOF: That's right.

CLARE: And how long have you worked for CERN?

FRITJOF: I don't.

CLARE: Oh.

FRITJOF: I am only visiting.

CLARE: Not part of the ...?

FRITJOF: No.

CLARE: Where do you ... what do you ...?

FRITJOF: I am a postdoctoral research associate ...

CLARE: Right.

FRITJOF: ... at the Institute of Particle and Nuclear Physics at the University of ...

Silence.

CLARE: Sorry … at the University of …?

FRITJOF: I sensed you glazing over, so I just kind of tailed off.

CLARE: Yeah … I … sorry. Go on. You're a research associate at the University of … Oslo, is it?

FRITJOF: Oslo?

CLARE: Sorry … I just assumed because you were Swedish …

FRITJOF: Oslo is the capital of Norway.

CLARE: Oh. So … then … um … Helsinki?

FRITJOF: The University of Edinburgh.

CLARE: Oh! My sister lives in Edinburgh!

FRITJOF: Whereabouts?

CLARE: I have no idea. We don't get on so we don't talk.

FRITJOF: Okay. Thank you for the drink, but I really should get some …

CLARE: No! Don't …! Don't go to your room … don't … please … don't finish your drink and go to sleep. You have to help me.

FRITJOF: With what?

CLARE: I don't understand any of it.

FRITJOF: The Hadron Collider?

CLARE: Yes.

FRITJOF: Do you need to?

CLARE: A bit.

FRITJOF: You're writing an article on …?

CLARE: Yes.

FRITJOF: … the LHC …?

CLARE: Yes.

FRITJOF: … for tomorrow, I guess?

CLARE: Yes.

FRITJOF: And you think hitting on scientists in the hotel bar the night before …?

CLARE: Not scientists. One scientist. You. And I'm not hitting on …

FRITJOF: I know.

CLARE: Could you summarise in four words … a sentence …?

FRITJOF: It's a particle accelerator. I'm not going to do your homework for you.

CLARE: There's no need to be patronising.

FRITJOF: I apologise.

CLARE: You're a teacher … you're a professor …

FRITJOF: I'm a post-doctoral research …

CLARE: So how would you describe it to an undergrad … to someone interested in, but not au fait with …?

FRITJOF: It's the largest machine ever built.

CLARE: And …?

FRITJOF: Look … I'm sorry. I'm not very interested in …

CLARE: Oh … just … okay … sure, but …

FRITJOF: I'm not much of a hand-holder.

CLARE: Just a brief summation of the god-particle. That's all I …

FRITJOF: *(Grimace.)* 'The god-particle'.

CLARE: Is that not …?

FRITJOF: You're not going to find God in a supercollider.

CLARE: Okay.

FRITJOF: If you put that in your article prepare to be flamed in
the comments.

CLARE: Oh shit ... really?

FRITJOF: What was ...? Clare was it?

CLARE: Yes.

FRITJOF: That's right. No 'i'. What's your background, Clare?
You have a science degree?

CLARE: Yes, but ... in biology. Not physics.

FRITJOF: But you write for a science journal or ...?

CLARE: I'm a correspondent for an online ... not online ...
well, yes, online ... rather not the print edition ... for the
online blog of ... edition of the ... for the science section
of the ... online ... bloggery blog science blog ... *(Beat.)*
I am a journalist. I am a science correspondent. I write
for a London based broadsheet. I have been at the paper
for two years now ... two and a half ... but I still feel
very much a newbie. My job so far has involved cutting
and pasting from press releases ... churnalism, I guess
... cutting and pasting and reformatting in order to fit a
pre-existing article-template. Though not my first proper
reporting assignment ... it does feel like ... it feels like ...
it requires actual words to be written by me ... it requires
actual journalism. And I'm only here because the senior
correspondent's mother has had some form of stroke-
slash-paralysis and is unable to ... and I have a folder of
... folders of ... physics papers and cuttings from Wired
and New Scientist ... I have an email from a professor at
Imperial College that's supposed to explain ... supposed
to ... I have pamphlets and PDF files from CERN's press
department ... I have podcasts introduced by Professor
Brian Cox ... and I can't ... I can't understand a fucking
word of any of it. What I can grasp is that this is massive
... that this is important ... that this is the biggest scientific

endeavour since the moon-landing … and I have been entrusted by one of the oldest established newspapers in the world to report on it … the first draft of history … and I'm going to fuck it up.

FRITJOF: Clare.

CLARE: Yes?

FRITJOF: I'm going to bed.

CLARE: Right.

FRITJOF: Chop up the press release … there'll be another one tomorrow … swap in some synonyms … presto.

CLARE: I want it to be good.

FRITJOF: Yeah?

CLARE: I want to be good at my job.

FRITJOF: Well, that's different.

CLARE: It'll have my name on it … in perpetuity … words out there … bad words for all time … with my name on it. The hideously permanent internet. I can blame CERN for that too.

FRITJOF: You can blame CERN for the World Wide Web. It's not the same thing as the Internet.

CLARE: Accurate yet unhelpful – like calling aubergines a fruit.

FRITJOF: What would be helpful?

CLARE: I don't …

FRITJOF: I'm offering.

CLARE: Yeah?

FRITJOF: What do you want to know?

CLARE: Are they going to make a black hole?

FRITJOF: Possibly.

CLARE: Shitting hell.

FRITJOF: But it would be so uncomprehendingly small as to be unable to interact with the rest of the universe ... and it would collapse within a matter of milliseconds.

CLARE: Milliseconds?

FRITJOF: Well ... yoctoseconds would be closer to ...

CLARE: What's a yoctosecond?

FRITJOF: It's the time it takes for a quark to emit a gluon. It's about one septillionth of a second.

CLARE: You're fucking with me now.

FRITJOF: It's all actual stuff.

CLARE: This black hole will collapse?

FRITJOF: Yes.

CLARE: You're sure?

FRITJOF: Fairly certain.

CLARE: And if it doesn't?

FRITJOF: You're asking if I think you'll spontaneously combust. It's not going to happen. And if it did ... well, I'd say 'go with the moment'.

CLARE: What are the chances that we are all going to die?

FRITJOF: One hundred per cent. But not because of a black hole, and certainly not because of the LHC.

CLARE: Perhaps I should call my husband. I want to keep ... anything I talk about within the article ... I want to keep within ... you know ... the confines of human experience. Of everyday experience.

FRITJOF: No one is going to tear a hole in reality. But you should call your husband anyway.

CLARE: Why?

FRITJOF: Because it's nice to speak to the people you love.

CLARE: I shouldn't be drinking. We're trying to conceive.

FRITJOF: Because no one ever got pregnant drunk.

CLARE: Six units a week reduces a woman's fertility by around eighteen per cent. I haven't pissed on a stick today. He'll ask and I'll have to say I forgot ... that I don't know the Swiss word for pregnancy test ... that I've been drinking ... that I'm so full of physics and theories ... press releases and information packs ... that there's no space left for babies. *(Beat.)* I was secretly hoping the world might actually end, then I wouldn't have to write up the science behind the reasons why it didn't. *(Beat.)* Have you fallen out with your wife?

FRITJOF: A man can be alone in a bar.

CLARE: Sure. *(Beat.)* I guess something will have sunk in. And if not, I'll fudge the CERN press release ... hope I extract the salient points ... talk of the god-particle and I guess I'll just have to weather the below-the-line comments.

FRITJOF: Good luck with that.

CLARE: You put your name on something ... you put your work into the public sphere ... it's an open invitation for people to kick you in the tits.

FRITJOF: I could talk to Professor Higgs ... I mean, he might not go for it ... but I could mention it to him ... and he might give you ... I don't know ... an exclusive quote or something.

CLARE: Are you talking about ...?

FRITJOF: Peter Higgs.

CLARE: As in … Mister Boson?

FRITJOF: He's an Emeritus Professor at my university … part of the Institute for Particle and Nuclear Physics. His hotel room is next to mine.

CLARE: Well, that would be … that would be … yes … could you?

FRITJOF: Not now, obviously.

CLARE: No?

FRITJOF: Well … no … it's coming up to one o'clock and he's …

CLARE: Asleep?

FRITJOF: … seventy-nine years old. *(Beat.)* I'll ask him in the morning. When I see him. Over breakfast.

CLARE: Okay.

FRITJOF: Okay?

CLARE: Thank you. *(Pause.)* We could knock on his door. Lightly. He might be awake.

FRITJOF: In the morning.

CLARE: Okay. *(Beat.)* Do you want to get another bottle?

3.

Corridor.

CLARE: Are you awake, Professor Higgs?

FRITJOF: Shh.

CLARE: I can't hear … hang on … is that the TV …? Has he got the telly on?

FRITJOF: No, it's … that's the air-conditioning …

CLARE: The air-conditioning?

FRITJOF: … or the heating.

CLARE: It's voices.

FRITJOF: It's not voices.

CLARE: It is.

FRITJOF: From upstairs, maybe?

CLARE: I should've brought a glass.

FRITJOF: A glass?

CLARE: A pint glass … to hold against the door.

FRITJOF: It would be a litre.

CLARE: What?

FRITJOF: We're in Switzerland.

CLARE: This is the room?

FRITJOF: He's fast asleep.

CLARE: I'm going to knock.

FRITJOF: Don't knock.

CLARE: Just lightly.

FRITJOF: Not even lightly.

CLARE: I could … I could … push something over … a water cooler …

FRITJOF: What?

CLARE: Make some noise … accidental … wake him up …

FRITJOF: I'm not going to wake him up.

CLARE: I bet he's excited. I bet he can't sleep. It's a big day for him tomorrow. It's like Christmas and birthday and …

FRITJOF: Please …

CLARE: Professor Higgs?

FRITJOF: Stop it.

CLARE: Professor Higgs?

FRITJOF: Come away.

CLARE: I'm going to start a small fire.

FRITJOF: Stop!

CLARE: Wake up, Peter Higgs! *(Listens.)* Nothing.

FRITJOF: Come away from …

CLARE: Wake up, Peter Higgs!

FRITJOF: He's obviously sound asleep …

CLARE: Wake up, Peter Higgs!

FRITJOF: Maybe he's taken something … a sleeping pill.

CLARE: Are you going to stand there or …?

FRITJOF: Wake up, Peter Higgs!

CLARE: Wake up, Peter Higgs! *(Listens.)* Still nothing.

FRITJOF: Wake up, Peter Higgs!

CLARE: Wake up, Peter Higgs!

4.

Office.

HERTA: This is your passport?

FRITJOF: It is.

HERTA: And this is yours?

CLARE: Can I have that back, please?

HERTA: You are in room 183?

FRITJOF: That is correct.

HERTA: And you are in room 250?

CLARE: Yes.

HERTA: What is the nature of your stay?

CLARE: The nature …?

HERTA: You are here on business?

CLARE: Yes.

HERTA: You are not here on your hen party?

CLARE: No.

HERTA: You are not here on some jolly wheeze?

CLARE: I am here for work.

HERTA: Your behaviour is not professional.

CLARE: I would like my passport.

FRITJOF: We are sorry for any disturbance.

HERTA: What line of work are you in, Mr Karlsson?

FRITJOF: I am a physicist.

HERTA: We get a lot of physicists here.

FRITJOF: I can imagine.

HERTA: I have worked in many hotels, Mr Karlsson. Many hotels across Europe. Riga. Prague. Amsterdam. I know how to deal with rowdy behaviour. I know how to deal with the English.

CLARE: Excuse me?

FRITJOF: I am sure.

CLARE: I am sorry that we made a noise … we won't be …

HERTA: I am talking to Mr Karlsson.

CLARE: But ...

HERTA: Mr Karlsson ...

CLARE: Doctor Karlsson.

HERTA: Is that right? Is it Doctor Karlsson?

FRITJOF: It doesn't matter.

HERTA: Are you also a doctor?

CLARE: No.

HERTA: The collider brings us business. Our proximity to the collider ... especially at this time ... brings good business to this hotel. But you scientists do not own us.

FRITJOF: No.

HERTA: You cannot barrel up and down our corridors, whooping and yelling like the Rolling Stones.

FRITJOF: I understand that.

HERTA: We have other customers. We have other guests.

FRITJOF: Of course.

HERTA: They are sleeping.

FRITJOF: Yes.

HERTA: Perhaps you do not sleep. Perhaps you keep unusual hours in your lab. Perhaps you are like a nocturnal creature that lives underground. Are you a nocturnal creature, Doctor Karlsson?

FRITJOF: No.

HERTA: You are in room 250.

CLARE: I am.

HERTA: And you are in room 183.

FRITJOF: Correct.

HERTA: You are married?

CLARE: Not to each other.

HERTA: I ask you to keep the noise down.

FRITJOF: We will.

HERTA: Very good. *(Beat.)* We take security very seriously.

FRITJOF: Do you consider us a threat to security?

CLARE: For making a bit of noise?

HERTA: Tomorrow is a big day.

CLARE: So … because of the LHC … you're at an elevated security level?

HERTA: We have been advised to remain vigilant. *(Beat.)* Would you please empty your pockets.

CLARE: Excuse me?

HERTA: Please.

CLARE: I'm not sure you have the authority to …

HERTA: Empty your pockets. Please. Thank you.

CLARE: On what authority do you …?

HERTA: I am the manager of this hotel.

CLARE: But you're not the police.

HERTA: I am asking politely.

CLARE: And I am declining. Politely.

HERTA: I can call security if you wish.

CLARE: Do they have the authority to riffle through …?

HERTA: I would like you to empty your pockets.

CLARE: I would like my passport back.

HERTA: I can ask you to leave.

CLARE: I am a journalist.

HERTA: Your threats are meaningless. We have a very favourable rating on TripAdvisor.

CLARE: I'm going back to my room.

HERTA: I can have you escorted from the grounds.

CLARE: You're ridiculous. *(Empties pockets.)* Room key. Gum. Bank card. Mobile phone. Not that it's any of your business.

HERTA: Thank you.

CLARE: There will be a letter of complaint.

HERTA: That is your right.

CLARE: I will publish it on my employer's website. 35 million unique users every month. I will also publish a fully referenced and hyper-linked version on my personal blog.

HERTA: As you wish.

CLARE: My social media presence reaches thousands.

HERTA: I am pleased for you. Sir?

FRITJOF: No.

HERTA: Will you empty your pockets, sir?

FRITJOF: No.

HERTA: Will you empty your pockets?

FRITJOF: No.

HERTA: Sir?

CLARE: What do you think we have? Do you think we're high? Do you think we have drugs?

HERTA: No one mentioned drugs.

CLARE: Do you think our clothes are lined with plastic explosives?

HERTA: No.

CLARE: Perhaps I'm wearing a wire. Do you think I'm wearing a wire?

HERTA: Why would you be wearing a wire?

CLARE: I don't know. You tell me. What have you done?

HERTA: Would you like me to call security?

CLARE: No one here is being threatened. What did you expect to find in my pockets? If you want gum, ask for gum.

HERTA: I do not want gum.

CLARE: What do you think you'll find in his?

HERTA: You were causing a disturbance. Do you deny this?

FRITJOF: No.

HERTA: Miss?

CLARE: No.

HERTA: It is reasonable to ask what you have in your pockets. *(Beat.)* You are turning on your machine tomorrow, yes?

FRITJOF: It is not my machine.

HERTA: But you are here for …?

FRITJOF: Yes, yes …

CLARE: … for the throwing of the switch.

HERTA: I like science.

FRITJOF: That is good to hear.

HERTA: I like Neil deGrasse Tyson. I like Carl Sagan.

FRITJOF: I like them too.

HERTA: But you are not out amongst the stars, Doctor
Karlsson, you are underground in burrows and tunnels.

FRITJOF: I'm at a desk most of the time.

HERTA: You concern yourself with tiny things.

FRITJOF: With theoretical things.

HERTA: Is there much distance between the theoretical and
the very small?

FRITJOF: I suppose not.

HERTA: I hope that while you're here you will enjoy the many
sights of Geneva and its surrounds. You are staying long?

FRITJOF: No.

HERTA: You?

CLARE: No.

HERTA: That is a shame. Geneva really does have a lot to
offer.

5.

Hotel room.

CLARE: The bar is closed. Can we order room service?
Will they bring us some beer?

FRITJOF: Is that going to help with your article?

CLARE: I can write drunk. I'm at my most creative when
drunk. I'm Hunter S. Thompson. I'm Don Draper.

FRITJOF: There's always the minibar.

CLARE: The minibar is a trap.

FRITJOF: I thought you had an expense account?

CLARE: Let's crack that bitch open. I haven't had dinner.

FRITJOF: Neither have I.

CLARE: It's not good to skip meals.

FRITJOF: We should probably eat something.

CLARE: Are you hungry?

FRITJOF: No.

CLARE: I can't say that surprises me. If I was raised on a diet of meatballs and rye bread, I probably wouldn't be all that interested in food either.

FRITJOF: That's hardly representative of …

CLARE: Dude, I've eaten in Ikea.

FRITJOF: You should try gravlax.

CLARE: Is that raw salmon?

FRITJOF: Cured salmon. And dill.

CLARE: Dill is for fools.

FRITJOF: You should at least try it before …

CLARE: I'm not going to eat anything that sounds like it should be fighting Doctor Who. *(Beat.)* So what's in your pockets? You got to see the contents of mine. I understand not wanting to show her … principle of the thing an' all … invasion of privacy …

FRITJOF: Why do you care?

CLARE: Because you were interestingly adamant about it.

FRITJOF: 'Interestingly adamant'?

CLARE: You woke up the journalist.

FRITJOF: I'm not going to empty my pockets.

CLARE: No?

FRITJOF: No.

CLARE: Well … if you won't distract me, you're going to have to help me. Why is it called the God-particle?

FRITJOF: It's not.

CLARE: Yes it is.

FRITJOF: It's really not.

CLARE: Then tell me why.

FRITJOF: There was a physicist … Leon Lederman … he was writing a book about the history of particle physics … the history of the Higgs' boson. He wanted to call it the 'goddamn-particle', because no one could find the fucker … but his publisher thought that might cause offence so they took out the 'damn'.

CLARE: He was probably working to a wordcount. *(Beat.)* I hate journalism. I hate press releases. I hate opinion pieces. You're either a parrot, a robot or a battery hen. I just wanted to go out into the world … with a notebook … investigate … record some interviews on my phone and write something … but this is just cold soup. I wanted to be Lois Lane … or Katharine Hepburn in *His Girl Friday* … I wanted to be *All the President's Men*. I still do. What I'm not built for is this. All that's required is that I generate traffic. It's not about truth or story or making something. And I don't have opinions … or rather the opinions I have are subject to change … and that's no use to anyone … my editor … anyone.

FRITJOF: If an opinion isn't subject to change, you can hardly call it an opinion – it just becomes a lie you tell yourself. Something you repeat to keep your world from falling apart.

CLARE: Why is it so important that we find this boson?

FRITJOF: It's not.

CLARE: It's six billion pounds of important.

FRITJOF: The universe doesn't care if we know how it works.

CLARE: I see. You're one of those 'because the sun's going to expand and swallow the earth in four billion years … everything is therefore meaningless' kind of people. Leave the Ladybird Book of Nihilism on the shelf and tell me something real.

FRITJOF: Light has no mass, but it does have momentum. The speed of light is the maximum speed that light can travel, but it can be slowed down. As it passes through atmospheres. As it passes through water. You could hold it in your hand. You could slow light down and hold it in your hand.

CLARE: *(Kisses him.)*

FRITJOF: *(No response.)*

CLARE: I didn't … I'm sorry …

FRITJOF: There's no need to apologise.

CLARE: I didn't kiss you because you're smart.

FRITJOF: Okay.

CLARE: I'm not trying to make myself smarter by kissing you … by association … by osmosis …

FRITJOF: Biology degree.

CLARE: Tick. I just … I just … it felt important to say that. I don't know why.

They kiss. These are the first new lips either of them have kissed in some years. It is awkward because their lips are expecting to kiss different mouths. But passion is soon remembered. There we go. That's it. Proper snogging now.

6.

Hotel room.

Both of them in a state of undress.

FRITJOF: Please don't apologise.

CLARE: It's just so …

FRITJOF: Probably for the best.

CLARE: … typical … of course … and gosh …

FRITJOF: Please don't be embarrassed.

CLARE: I'm not embarrassed.

FRITJOF: You have no need to be.

CLARE: Schoolgirls get embarrassed. They shouldn't, but they do.

FRITJOF: It was a bad idea.

CLARE: It's my body's way of saying 'no'.

FRITJOF: You have … everything you need?

CLARE: You can say 'tampon' – it's a perfectly good word.

FRITJOF: I know, but …

CLARE: … but …

FRITJOF: … but, yeah …

CLARE: I'm not one to be caught out. *(Pause.)* I do need to … I do need to apologise because … I have a limited vocabulary of action. I am sorry for that. You've been kind … you've been helpful … sometimes that's how people say thank you … how I say thank you … or used to. Or we can call it a distraction … procrastination … a procrastination fuck. Jesus. So … for that … sorry.

FRITJOF: We stopped before anything really …

CLARE: Well … we were cock-blocked by womb-lining. It's the same thing, I suppose.

FRITJOF: I guess now you don't need that pregnancy test.

CLARE: I guess not.

Awkward silence.

FRITJOF: This isn't getting your article written.

CLARE: No.

FRITJOF: What are you going to do?

CLARE: Write something terrible. It doesn't matter. It'll just be lost in the noise. There must be a thousand pages a day uploaded to that website. One article of mediocre quality … one beige, poorly researched soft turd of a piece amongst the rest … who's going to notice? And if they do … if those that know turn up to comment … turn up to pick apart … well, that's all ad-revenue. Why craft … why refine … why strive to be good … when you'll never see the shark for the suckerfish? *(Beat.)* He wants a child so much. And we've been trying. We've been trying … for what feels like … but my life is full … my time is full … do you understand? My days are full. I am full. To the brim. I've got books on how to declutter your life – hundreds of them. For him there's a space to be filled. *(Beat.)* Do you have kids?

FRITJOF: We talked about it.

CLARE: Do you think you ever will?

FRITJOF: Not now, no.

CLARE: How does your wife feel about that?

FRITJOF: Clare … my wife died …

CLARE: Oh … I … oh …

FRITJOF: … not quite a year ago.

CLARE: I am so …

FRITJOF: Don't … don't … it's … I'm okay. I've got support … a support network. I've got friends and work colleagues. Everyone's been very kind. *(Beat.)* She loved this whole endeavour … the Hadron Collider. The logistics of it. She was an engineer. We met when she was a postgraduate student. She was fascinated by the LHC as a … as a building project. As construction. The tunnelling … the earthworks.

CLARE: How did she die?

FRITJOF: *(Silence.)*

CLARE: I shouldn't have … I shouldn't have asked …

FRITJOF: You can ask. I don't mind the asking. I just have to decide if I want to answer or not. *(Beat.)* That was the first … yours are the first lips … since my wife.

CLARE: Oh god … I am so sorry.

FRITJOF: No … it's fine … it's good. Because there are bound to be other kisses … other lips. I'm not an idiot, I'm young still. There will be other loves. It's less of a betrayal to throw it away – we both agree it was throwaway – than to burden any prospective future relationship with …

CLARE: Yeah … no … of course.

FRITJOF: I grew up in a town called Kiruna … in northern Sweden. It's a landscape of iron ore … of mining and natural mineral resource. A mine towers over the town … the excavated earth … black and a heap … like the corpse of a giant dragged from beneath the ground and left to calcify on the surface. You can take tours … they conduct tours … down into the pit … there's a lift that takes you down … and whenever I took her home … whenever we visited … we would take the lift and we would walk the miles of mineshaft. So much hollow … so much empty … you'd think the world was a honeycomb. *(Beat.)* Professor

Higgs ... as a kindness ... offered to bring me with ...
so of course I accepted ... of course. He wasn't to know
that it would feel like a betrayal ... to be heading under the
ground tomorrow ... into those hollows. It feels something
like a betrayal.

CLARE: I'm sure she wouldn't ...

FRITJOF: Don't. Please. Thank you. *(Beat.)* She had hereditary
angioedema ... it causes random swellings in the ... in the
extremities, the face, the gastrointestinal tract ... in the ...
in the airways ...

CLARE: Okay.

FRITJOF: ... she had to undergo surgery when ... but ...

CLARE: *(Takes his hand.)*

FRITJOF: The LHC ... the vacuum of the collider ... is said to
be the emptiest place in the solar system ... emptier than
interplanetary space. That can't be right. *(Pause.)* I think we
should call it a night. I think we should ...

CLARE: Yeah, sure ... of course ... here let me ...

*CLARE starts gathering up FRITJOF's clothes to pass to him.
One item is unusually heavy.*

CLARE: Hmm.

FRITJOF: What is it?

CLARE: It's just ... nothing ... only ... this has a peculiar
weight.

7.

Kitchen.

FRITJOF: I need a bigger pan. I really need a much bigger pan.

CLARE: How many eggs?

FRITJOF: I don't need eggs.

CLARE: Yes, you need eggs.

FRITJOF: I need corn-flour.

CLARE: You can't make custard without breaking eggs.

FRITJOF: I need corn-flour and water and I don't really need that much else.

CLARE: Well that sounds delicious.

FRITJOF: It's not meant to be delicious … it's meant to be illustrative.

CLARE: When you say custard, you mean custard made from powdered custard?

FRITJOF: Yeah.

CLARE: I'm not sure this is the sort of establishment that'll keep a box of custard powder to hand – they serve their desserts on slate. Will it work if we make it from scratch?

FRITJOF: I'm a theorist … you're asking the wrong guy.

CLARE: Here's a pan. Now we need a whisk. Talk to me about custard.

FRITJOF: Custard – as any fool knows – is a non-Newtonian liquid. Meaning that it doesn't act as water does. If you were to run at a lake of custard, the impact of your foot would cause the surface to momentarily increase in viscosity … momentarily solidify … so much so that it would support your weight as you peg it over to the other side. Stop or slow down and you would begin to sink into the crème anglaise and die a painful and gently vanilla-flavoured death. The Higgs field is custard. Photons – light – gathers no custard … has no mass. It skims across the Higgs' field as fast as any particle can – the speed limit of the universe – that's why that speed limit is known as the speed of light.

CLARE: *(Finds a whisk and a useful bowl.)* I've found a whisk. Check the fridges for eggs.

FRITJOF: So why don't all particles travel at that same speed? Why don't you and I … why don't these walls … this flooring …? Why isn't this hotel a cloud? Why isn't everything in the universe just a haze of unconnected particles tearing around at the very limit of light? Why does anything have weight? Why does mass exist? What is mass? What brings us together? We don't know. We guess some particles aren't travelling fast enough, so they get bogged down. But by what? Higgs' theoretical custard.

CLARE: I can't use that.

FRITJOF: No?

CLARE: Who the hell knows you can run across custard? No one knows that.

FRITJOF: You can see people doing it all over YouTube.

FRITJOF opens a fridge. CLARE opens a cupboard. In the fridge there is a large tub of fresh custard. In the cupboard is a large tub of powdered custard.

CLARE: Jackpot.

FRITJOF: Same.

They prise the lids off their tubs.

CLARE: Show me then.

FRITJOF brings his tub to the centre. CLARE still holds hers. FRITJOF pours his liquid custard into the useful bowl.

FRITJOF: Liquid … agreed?

CLARE: Agreed.

FRITJOF: The harder I hit this … the faster I am … the more energy … the more solid it will become. Okay?

CLARE: Okay.

FRITJOF: Okay.

FRITJOF lifts his hand and brings it down heavily on the surface of the custard. His fist bounces off.

CLARE is amazed.

FRITJOF punches the custard again. It's a little imperfect as an experiment and some custard splashes. CLARE laughs.

They take turns slapping, punching, slopping the custard. The experiment falls apart and they are now just joyfully playing.

FRITJOF lobs some custard at her. CLARE throws a handful of custard powder at him. They both laugh. He lobs some more. So does she.

Custard fight!

8.

Office.

HERTA: The kitchen is off limits to guests.

CLARE: We understand that.

FRITJOF: We will pay for any costs.

CLARE: Absolutely.

HERTA: It is the inconsideration. For the property. For the chef. For the cleaning staff.

FRITJOF: We understand.

HERTA: If you understood you would not be here ... in front of me ... in this office.

CLARE: We understand now.

HERTA: Hindsight is a remarkable thing.

FRITJOF: You are within your rights to ask us to leave.

HERTA: I am.

FRITJOF: But ... it is ... it is 4am ...

CLARE: Is it 4am?

FRITJOF: It is. We will pay for any costs. We will leave quietly in the morning.

HERTA: It is within my rights to call the police also.

CLARE: Oh come on …!

FRITJOF: There's no need for …

HERTA: I could suggest a charge of property damage.

CLARE: We didn't 'damage' anything.

HERTA: The custard is despoiled. It cannot be served now.

FRITJOF: Do you think the police will be interested in such a charge?

HERTA: Will you return to your rooms?

FRITJOF: Yes.

HERTA: Will you remain there?

FRITJOF: Yes.

HERTA: You will not be welcome back at this hotel. Do you understand that?

FRITJOF: We do.

HERTA: This hotel does not exist in some sort of repercussion-proof bubble.

FRITJOF: Again, we apologise for any disturbance caused.

HERTA: Apologies are all very well, but if the price of such disturbance can be met with words alone then …

CLARE: Then …?

HERTA: *(Shrugs.)*

CLARE: Hardly the end of the world, I think.

HERTA: And that is why the world is as it is.

CLARE: *(To FRITJOF.)* Do you have your wallet on you?

FRITJOF: Why?

CLARE: I only have a bank card. I'll pay you back.

FRITJOF: *(Hands over wallet.)*

CLARE: *(Takes money from wallet and places it in front of HERTA.)*

HERTA: What is this?

CLARE: Two hundred Swiss Francs.

HERTA: What do you expect me to do with it?

CLARE: *(Shrugs.)*

HERTA: *(Not impressed.)*

FRITJOF: *(Puts the money back in his wallet.)*

HERTA: It is too easy to throw around money and apologies. They often weigh the same.

FRITJOF: We didn't mean to insult you.

HERTA: I do not do this job because I like people, Doctor Karlsson. I do not enjoy this. I do not wish to interact with society. I want society to be tucked up asleep in their allotted rooms. A tick-box sheet of breakfast items hung on a door handle is all the human interaction I require. And yet … here I find myself presented with an opportunity. An opportunity for education. You must learn cost. Two hundred francs is seemingly nothing to you … an apology is seemingly nothing to you … a lifetime ban from this hotel also the same. I cannot say that I know you well, Doctor Karlsson, but there is one thing that I have seen that is a sticking point … and so to that I must return … so that you may understand consequence. Will you please empty your pockets?

CLARE: Oh my god.

HERTA: Doctor Karlsson?

CLARE: You don't have to do anything.

FRITJOF acquiesces. He pulls from his pocket the rectangle of glass. Daylight pours from it. Eerie and beautiful. Light fills the room. We never knew how dark it was before this light.

9.

Hotel room.

FRITJOF: Light has no mass, but it does have momentum. The speed of light is the maximum speed that light can travel. But it can be slowed down. As it passes through atmospheres. As it passes through water. This ... this is Slow Glass. It is transparent ... light flows through it ... but at a greatly reduced speed. This piece ... it takes roughly ten years for light to pass through.

CLARE: It's not an iPad.

FRITJOF: No.

CLARE: She thought it was an iPad.

FRITJOF: She knows of iPads. She doesn't know of this. And so this unknowable thing ... which sits outside of her experience ... outside her frame of reference ... it is easier to replace it in her mind with something that she does know. It is always easier to believe what you already believe.

CLARE: It's heavy.

FRITJOF: Yes.

CLARE: It's cold. What is it made of?

FRITJOF: When you start closely packing atoms together ... at incredibly low temperatures ... in a vacuum ... matter can enter a pretty exotic state. As light travels through such a complex and dense material ... well, it slows down ... it takes on more physical properties. You could almost touch it ... almost hold it in your hands. Pick the light out of the air … turn it over in your fingers … mould it … shape it … make something new. In 1998 a team at Harvard slowed light down to around 38 miles per hour. The speed of light is normally 186,000 miles per second. Within two years that same team managed to bring light to a full stop.

CLARE: A full stop?

FRITJOF: And then they restarted it again. There are practical applications … in the fields of information storage … quantum computing and the like …

CLARE: This is daylight … old daylight … yesterdaylight …?

FRITJOF: You hold in your hands ten years' worth of light. You're looking at the past.

CLARE: How did you get this?

FRITJOF: I knew someone working on a research team.

CLARE: At Harvard?

FRITJOF: No. This is from somewhere else. Somewhere less public. It was meant to be destroyed. Instead he sent it to me.

CLARE: Why isn't this stuff everywhere?

FRITJOF: Too expensive to manufacture … difficult to apply to a practical purpose … the Illuminati … who knows?

CLARE: There's movement.

FRITJOF: Yeah.

CLARE: What am I looking at?

FRITJOF: I receive this message out of nowhere … from an old friend … a colleague. He'd fallen off the radar … had lost contact. Friends drift apart, we all know this. And this message … a letter … well, a postcard in an envelope … it simply says: 'I am sending you something'. No return address. No pleasantries. I don't even know how he knew where I lived. I mention it to my wife. She pulls a quizzical

face … I shrug my shoulders … we have a little chuckle at
the weirdness of it. The card goes in the recycling.
A month later we receive a delivery … UPS or ParcelForce,
nothing odd … she signs for this box. Not a big box, but
it is heavy. No bigger than a three ream pack of A4, but
the guy needs to use his trolley to get it from the van to
the house. When I get home – I've been doing the weekly
shop – it's about four o'clock in the afternoon but it's
winter and Edinburgh, so you know: dark – I come into the
front room … and there is daylight. The brightest noonday
sun. My wife is sat in the middle of the floor surrounded
by these tiles … these tiles of sunlight … all fanned out in
a spiral. She doesn't say anything … she's just grinning …
that innocent 'let's fly a kite' grin that you can't hide …
that you can't stop yourself from smiling. I pick one of the
tiles up and I'm looking at it … I'm looking at it … and
it's wrong … it's strange … it's a landscape … a window
onto a landscape … of mountains and trees and sky. I turn
it over in my hands … and it's Slow Glass. It's Slow Glass.
I explain it to her … I explain how light can be slowed
down and stored … how this theoretical material is now
very much not theoretical but here … in our front room.
We spread it out … link up the image … like a jigsaw.
We have some grout leftover … because we'd not long
done up the bathroom and she had become a dab-hand
self-taught tiler. That night … that same night … we're
covering one of the walls in our front room with these tiles
of Slow Glass. It was living wallpaper. It was a portal to
another dimension. Our best guess is that the view was of
somewhere in Upstate New York … the Appalachians …
oak, maple and spruce. Whatever the drizzle … whatever
the Scottish drizzle outside … the flame of those Autumn
North American colours filled our front room … the bright
blue sky … the clearest days. And the wildlife … the birds
of prey … the deer … in our front room … separated from
us by a pane of glass and ten years. I remember we were
sat on the sofa one night … boxsetting our lives away …
and this … this *immense* electrical storm broke out across
the Slow Glass. Lightning without thunder. Sheets of rain.

Trees bending in gales. And neither of us paying attention
to the TV anymore … just hands and fingers interlocked
… a head on a shoulder … the smell of her … the cocoa-
butter on her skin … her hair-products. I'm … I'm sorry …
(Beat.) Even now … just thinking about … it brings back
that arrhythmia of love … that shimmer down one side
of the heart … this fucking phantom limb. *(Beat.)* No one
takes pictures at funerals. No one hires a photographer. I
can't really remember the day … it is all blurs and stabs.
So now, when I see people … friends … family people …
I have to ask them 'were you there?' Because I don't know.
And no one took a photograph. *(Beat.)* I functioned fairly
well those first few weeks … fed myself … though I threw
away a lot of off-milk. And then … one day I came home
and our house was dark. And our house was *never* dark. We
had a wormhole in space and time on our living room wall.
But the tiles were black. It never occurred to me that they
would run out. Of course the light would end. I cried more
on that day than on any other. I avoided the front room
for a while … ate in the kitchen … I spent some nights
at the Premier Inn down the road. Anything to get away
from those spent tiles. But then … with drink in my system
… one day I found myself reaching for my toolbox. The
hammer smacked against the wall … cracking the tiles …
breaking them … a chip … a splinter. I dug the claw-teeth
into the grouting and pulled a section from the wall. The
room filled with light again … like a punch to the throat.
The light … from the rear side of the broken glass. I picked
it up and held it to my eye. And there she was. There was
Marie … youthful and beautiful … ten years younger.
All those tiles … all of those tiles … the light of the past
decade … all of that love … stored in those glass tiles.
(Beat.) Here she comes. Coming home. She'll get some
water from the kitchen and come back … stand in front
of the Slow Glass wall for a moment. She's looking at
that landscape. It won't even occur to her that I could be
watching from ten years in her future. Just light bouncing
around the universe … landing on this … reflecting off that
… perhaps seen, probably not. *(pause)* Rosalind Russell.

CLARE: Excuse me?

FRITJOF: It was Rosalind Russell in *His Girl Friday*. The Hepburn film you're most probably thinking of is *Woman of the Year* ... opposite Spencer Tracy. Sorry. It's been bugging me ever since you said it.

CLARE: You knew what I was getting at.

FRITJOF: I suppose so. I didn't mean to ...

CLARE: It's fine.

FRITJOF: What time is it?

CLARE: It's late. Or early.

FRITJOF: Depending on how you look at it.

CLARE: Where did you say you were from? The north of Sweden?

FRITJOF: That's right.

CLARE: The northern lights.

FRITJOF: In the winter, yes.

CLARE: I've never seen them. I'd love to. They're on my list.

FRITJOF: They photograph better than they look. *(Beat.)* Kiruna ... where I grew up ... all that industry ... all that tunnelling ... it has literally undermined the town. To the extent that the ground is so thin, there's a real danger of collapse ... of the city centre collapsing into the mines beneath. The ground is weak now. They are moving the town two miles to the East. Homes relocated ... businesses ... in case the ground opens up and swallows them all. Its entire centre is shifting. Will we even be able to call it the same place?

CLARE: You'll go down into the tunnels?

FRITJOF: Tomorrow?

CLARE: Well, later today.

FRITJOF: I suppose so.

CLARE: Will it still feel like a betrayal?

FRITJOF: *(Does not answer.)*

CLARE: Do you want to know what I think? I think you
cannot betray someone you've lost. Because you cannot
go through the experience of losing someone and come
out unchanged. They would have never known the you
that underwent that process of grief. They never knew you
as you are now, with that hurt in your heart. And that's
okay. That's okay. The person that they knew died with
them. *(Deep breath.)* The world's largest and most powerful
machine was switched on for the first time today. Costing
upwards of five billion pounds, the Large Hadron Collider
– LHC – straddles the Swiss-French border. The particle
accelerator resides within 27 kilometres of tunnels and has
taken nearly thirty years to build. The scientists hope to
recreate conditions similar to the first few moments after
the Big Bang in an effort to discover the elusive God-
particle. Two beams of subatomic particles – protons – will
be fired at each other at speeds approaching the speed of
light. The LHC is a partnership between the twenty-two
member states of CERN. Founded in 1954, CERN was
one of the first pan-European initiatives, endeavouring to
promote scientific and cultural collaboration and exchange.
TV's Professor Brian Cox said he was thrilled at the results
and thought that the LHC was 'just amazing'. Black-hole
boffin, Stephen Hawking, said something inspiring in his
cool robot voice.

FRITJOF: That'll do.

CLARE: You think?

FRITJOF: Yeah.

CLARE: I want it to be good.

FRITJOF: Does it matter?

CLARE: I want it to matter.

FRITJOF: The only things that have meaning are those that we ascribe meaning to.

CLARE: I know. And some things fall apart before they even begin. And it's possible to feel loss for something you never wanted. And we'll all be forgotten, and the sun will swallow the earth and the universe will die. But you can't live your life like that, can you? Can you?

10.

Lobby.

FRITJOF: Good morning.

CLARE: Hi.

FRITJOF: Did you manage to sleep?

CLARE: I managed about an hour.

FRITJOF: Are you heading down to breakfast?

CLARE: I was just going to get some juice.

FRITJOF: I haven't seen Professor Higgs yet this morning, so I haven't asked him for …

CLARE: Don't worry about it.

FRITJOF: Are you sure?

CLARE: It's fine. I don't think I need it.

FRITJOF: Okay.

CLARE: I've got my three hundred words.

FRITJOF: Yeah?

CLARE: I've been up since six.

FRITJOF: Oh, well done.

CLARE: Coffee is my friend.

FRITJOF: Are you happy with it?

CLARE: Yes. I think so. Yes.

FRITJOF: I can still get a quote …?

CLARE: There will be enough things said today. There will be
a press release.

FRITJOF: If the world doesn't end.

CLARE: Yeah.

FRITJOF: So …

CLARE: It doesn't, though, does it?

FRITJOF: No.

CLARE: There's a bus picking up all the press …

FRITJOF: Right.

CLARE: … in front of the hotel in about half an hour. I need to
brush my teeth and check out.

FRITJOF: You haven't brushed your teeth?

CLARE: I've not drunk any juice yet. I'm not an animal.
I'm probably not going to get a chance to …

FRITJOF: What?

CLARE: Thank you.

She hugs him. A tight hug. One that says goodbye to an old friend.

CLARE: Well, you take care of yourself.

FRITJOF: You too.

CLARE's mobile phone rings. She looks at the screen.

FRITJOF: Your husband?

CLARE: *(Nods.)*

FRITJOF: *(A little wave goodbye.)*

CLARE: *(Answers her phone.)* Morning. Yeah … I'm just heading down to breakfast. Did you sleep well? I miss you. *(Exits.)*

FRITJOF: *(Alone, he pulls the pane of Slow Glass from his pocket, he looks at it, he doesn't need to look anymore, so he puts it away.)*

MYTH

Characters

SARAH – mid to late thirties
GEORGE – late twenties
LAURA – mid to late thirties
TOM – late thirties, early forties

About the play

Myth *is a play in which the real narrative emerges from
the actors, not the characters they are playing. During the
action we meet four actors playing the parts of: Sarah,
George, Laura, and Tom, but really this story belongs to
the actor playing Sarah. We see the world more and more
from her POV, as the play progresses and their constructed
world begins to fall apart. Throughout the action the
actors will face challenges that are sometimes part of
the scene itself, sometimes part of the performance of the
scene, and sometimes part of the outside world at large,
which begins to interfere more and more with the action.
But only the actor playing Sarah really acknowledges
the noises, oil, and objects that interfere with the action.
As the obstacles escalate the actor playing Sarah becomes
more and more visible as she finds it harder and harder
to keep the fiction going and stay in role. The actors
playing Tom, Laura and George are aware of Sarah's
odd behavior but oblivious to the cause. It's not that they
can't physically see what's happening; they just choose
not to really look at it. Aside from assisting the actor
playing Sarah with her forgotten cues and doing what
they can to keep the narrative running, they will continue
as normal. No matter what happens, Sarah's colleagues
carry on as though nothing was wrong. They must keep
the performance going.*

No delegations have been made in this copy of the script to indicate when the performers come out of character and speak the lines simply as themselves. Likewise, we have not specified when the lines relate to the situation within the 'play' and when they refer to the wider situation that unfolds around the action. These decisions are for you to make.

This text is a copy of the original production's staging, within it various physical elements are referenced i.e oil soaked birds – each company can choose to replicate these elements or introduce their own at these points in the script.

The set for Myth *should clearly be a set. Whilst attempting to replicate a stylish Victorian terrace home, we as an audience are aware that we are in a theatre.*

A1.

GEORGE and SARAH's living room/kitchen. East London. They have only been here two weeks, and this is evidenced by several boxes that have yet to be unpacked. A couple of Ikea bags spill their contents out onto the floor. Waitrose bags sit on the kitchen counters, partially unpacked. Despite the mess, it is clear that in time it will be a very chic and stylish home.

GEORGE is rooting around in the packing boxes, clearly looking for something and failing to find it. SARAH enters, flustered. She has a shopping bag with her.

SARAH: Sorry sorry sorry, I know I'm late!! It's taken me *literally* forever to get home.

GEORGE: They'll be here in fifteen minutes.

SARAH: I know I know. I said, I'm sorry.

GEORGE: What happened?

SARAH: Err, what happened is that we moved so far out of town that by the time I get home at night it's practically time to turn around and go back to work.

GEORGE continues to rummage, finally finding some plates and unpacking them onto the kitchen counter.

GEORGE: Right.

SARAH: Seriously, you can make that noise but you don't have to do my journey. It's complete fucking chaos out there. And as if it isn't bad enough on a normal day, tonight the tube just decides to stop dead /

GEORGE: Uh huh.

SARAH: /right in the middle of the tunnel. It just stopped there /

GEORGE: Uh huh.

SARAH: / for ages. Literally the worst journey ever. Are you even listening to me?

GEORGE: Yes. Yup. Definitely. Did you get the wine?

SARAH: I didn't have enough time to get to Waitrose so I had to go to the shop on the corner, which only stocks Echo Falls.

GEORGE: Oh well.

SARAH: Oh well? That is not the correct response to a full-blown booze crisis.

GEORGE: It's just wine.

SARAH: It's not just wine, it is an insult to wine!

She waves the one of the bottles under GEORGE's nose.

GEORGE: Oooh, fizzy!!

SARAH: Seriously. I'm thirty-seven, I shouldn't have to drink Echo Falls! And they'll be here in ten minutes. This is a massive fucking crisis.

GEORGE: Calm down!

SARAH: I will not calm down! I've just spent almost an hour trapped on the train from hell and I would quite like a drink that's not bloody Echo Falls.

GEORGE: You poor, poor thing.

SARAH: Oh piss off. Honestly, I've had a shitty evening. No one knew what was going on. They made no announcements. Not one! And we're all there crammed into the carriage. There's just too many people. There's no space. And we're all pit to pit and you know I've got a high metabolism so am prone to sweating. So I'm really at the mercy of the temperature, which by this point is getting obscene. I mean, it's *so hot*. February, it's meant to be bloody winter!

GEORGE: Which is why I'm so worried about Arthur.

SARAH: He'll show up, don't worry! Jesus, George, it's a fucking mess in here. What have you been doing all day?

GEORGE: I've had a very busy day as it happens!

SARAH clocks the Ikea bag.

SARAH: So I see.

She pulls out an unidentified kitchen implement.

SARAH: What the hell...?

GEORGE: I spent all morning trying to find the cutlery and roasting tins, and then I decided it would be quicker to just pop out and buy some more.

SARAH: Every box is labelled.

GEORGE: There's no mention of roasting tins on any boxes.

SARAH: KITCHEN. EQUIPMENT. I mean, what is this?

GEORGE: Garlic press. You know what it's like...you get to the bit past the show room, you know, where they keep all the funky stuff/

SARAH: The Marketplace.

GEORGE: Yup, The Marketplace. And somehow, before you know it, you end up with a trolley full of really cool stuff.

SARAH finds an apron and puts it on GEORGE.

SARAH: Mmmm. Really cool.

GEORGE: So I have had a very productive day thank you. And now it's wine o'clock, Echo Falls or not.

He pulls out a pack of wine glasses.

SARAH: We have wine glasses already!!

GEORGE: Yes, but not unpacked. I couldn't find them either. And these were four pounds. FOUR POUNDS!!

SARAH: Jesus Christ, they're in the box marked *glasses!*

Pointing at a box.

GEORGE: So you don't want a glass then.

SARAH: Yes. Fine. Why not. But it's also warm because they don't keep it in the fridge.

GEORGE: Oh wait. No. Wait until you see this!! Finally arrived, from Japan, I'll have you know.

GEORGE opens the freezer compartment and pulls out an ice cube tray which contains four huge circular balls of ice.

GEORGE: Ta da! This should do the trick. Look. I told you I'd had a productive day.

GEORGE has flipped a cube into each glass, it takes up most of the glass, SARAH shakes her head at GEORGE in disbelief, as she pops the bottle and pours. Meanwhile, GEORGE carries on with setting up dinner.

SARAH: Well actually, so have I. I've had a bit of news... And before they arrive I really need to talk –

GEORGE pulls out a chair from the table.

GEORGE: Arthur!! There you are you naughty boy!

GEORGE picks up a small brown box, which was on the chair. He listens, then says very quietly.

GEORGE: I think he's okay.

SARAH: Great. But can we –

GEORGE: Oh I've got so many things to show you when you wake up buddy. This is your new home!

SARAH: George!

GEORGE: Alright. I'll just pop him somewhere safe.

SARAH: Don't go wandering off when I'm trying to tell you something, just put him down there.

GEORGE places the box on the sofa.

GEORGE: Yes sorry, you were saying. A productive day.

SARAH: Well yes, apart from the bits I spent trapped on a tube carriage. But the reason I was late in the first place was –

The smoke alarm begins to go off.

GEORGE: Shit shit shit!!

GEORGE runs to the oven and pulls out a casserole, just in time.

GEORGE: Phew. Caught it.

GEORGE waves some packing in front of the smoke alarm until it stops.

GEORGE: Sorry. What were you saying about the reason you were late?

GEORGE continues to lay the table.

SARAH: Well, I. I had a meeting this afternoon, and something came up which meant we had to go to the pub and –

GEORGE: Say no more.

SARAH: But I –

GEORGE: No, I get it. Part and parcel of the job.

GEORGE has now disappeared off into the hall.

SARAH: No listen, it was…

GEORGE reappears holding an absolutely enormous shrub in a pot.

SARAH: What the *hell* is that?

GEORGE: It's a plant. I told you I'd had a productive –

SARAH: It's not a plant, it's a hedge you're putting a hedge on our dinner table.

GEORGE: I think it's rather handsome.

SARAH: You said you were getting flowers. It's not even a houseplant.

GEORGE: I like it.

SARAH: Well you seem to like living here /

GEORGE: Yes, I do.

SARAH: / in the middle of bloody nowhere, miles from the tube /

GEORGE: It's nice!

SARAH: / so your opinion is clearly warped.

Pause.

SARAH: Tell me it's going to be okay.

GEORGE: It's going to be okay.

SARAH: Remind me why on earth we moved here?

GEORGE: Was it because we could have a lovely home, yes, that could be the reason.

SARAH: A lovely home surrounded by shit wine and gang violence.

GEORGE: Sarah. Stop being so negative!

SARAH: I just didn't think this is where we'd end up.

GEORGE: I know. But isn't that amazing, we're on a true adventure, not knowing what the future has in store.

SARAH: Endless commutes, crowded buses, knife crime and gangs – that's our future.

GEORGE: And don't forget shit wine.

SARAH: Silly of me, how can I forget that.

SARAH smiles despite herself, she kisses GEORGE.

SARAH: Speaking of our future though –

Doorbell.

SARAH: It's not them already, is it?

GEORGE: It is that time.

SARAH: Ah, I'm not ready.

GEORGE: It'll be okay.

SARAH: This room is a mess!

GEORGE: Well we can't do anything about it now, can we?

> *GEORGE exits. SARAH finishes her drink. Looks at her phone. GEORGE returns, a skip in his step.*

GEORGE: Carry on, as you were. It's not them. Parcel.

SARAH: I can see that. What is it?

GEORGE: I don't know. The TV? The microwave? That record player you ordered from *eBay*.

SARAH: Don't shake it, just bloody open it!

> *They open the box. It's full of packaging.*

SARAH: Hurry up!

GEORGE: Okay.

SARAH: As if there wasn't enough crap in this room already! And we don't have time –

> *From the enormous box GEORGE pulls out a tiny kitchen implement.*

GEORGE: Fantastic!!

SARAH: What the hell is it?

GEORGE: A gnocchi griddle/

SARAH: You've got to be joking?

GEORGE: / you just put the gnocchi here, push it down, and it griddles it for you.

SARAH: We do not need this in our life.

GEORGE: Well that's what you think now, but this is going to change your gnocchi forev –

SARAH: Ah! You think you're being normal, but actually you're just enabling the end of civilization.

GEORGE: Darling, you've probably got time to get changed now.

SARAH: Oh. Do I look that bad?

GEORGE: No, not at all, you look great, but you know, it's a special occasion, I've put my shirt on.

SARAH: The shirt, yes you have.

GEORGE: And this is a very very special occasion.

SARAH: Oh. Is it?

GEORGE: Yes it is!

SARAH: In what way?

GEORGE: Well... I've not actually invited Adele and Paul round.

SARAH: But the table is set for four.

GEORGE: Indeed it is.

SARAH: I know that look. What's going on?

GEORGE: "OMG I love your new hair. It's been like this a while but thanks. It's been so long. I miss you so much. Completely. We must rectify this. Yeah, that is an amazing idea."

SARAH: Have you become bipolar in the last ten hours?

GEORGE: Does that not feel familiar? They're your words.

SARAH: My words?

GEORGE: Verbatim. On Facebook. To Laura.

SARAH: Laura?...do not say Laura Rainsford.

GEORGE: Yep, the one and only. Surprise!

SARAH: You're really telling me it's Laura Rainsford that's coming for dinner?!

GEORGE: And Tom.

SARAH: And fucking Tom!

58

GEORGE: You're making this sound less positive than I imagined.

SARAH: Less positive? This is like my worst nightmare.

GEORGE: Ah.

SARAH: What on earth were you thinking? And how, I mean, how have you even created this mess?

GEORGE: I saw her post on your Facebook page and you said catching up would be an amazing idea.

SARAH: I did not say that.

GEORGE: You did.

SARAH: No. I wrote that on Facebook.

GEORGE: Oh. Well. I thought you meant it, so I messaged her. From your account.

SARAH: From my account? You mean you *fraped* me?!!

GEORGE: Yes, but –

SARAH: And you invited her over!

GEORGE: Yes. And Tom.

SARAH: Oh yes, don't forget bloody Tom. How on earth could that have seemed like a good idea?!

GEORGE: I thought it would do you good to see some old friends.

SARAH: Well, we're not friends any more. We need to stop this now.

GEORGE: It's too late.

SARAH: It's never too late.

GEORGE: Actually, this time it is. They'll be here any minute.

SARAH: Why, why, why would you do this?

GEORGE: You've met all of my friends and I've not really met any of yours –

SARAH: There's a reason for that –

GEORGE: You're embarrassed about me?

SARAH: No, God no, of course I'm not embarrassed about you. I'm embarrassed about *them*: they're all arseholes, and these two are the most gaping ones of them all. They're just…they're from another time in my life.

GEORGE: Oh. I thought she was your best friend?

SARAH: She was… Once. Look, I've been avoiding her all year, hoping that if I bury my head in the sand she'll disappear. And now you, you've just invited her into our house! Tonight George, of all the nights when we really need to talk about –

Doorbell rings.

B1.

SARAH and GEORGE greet TOM and LAURA. TOM is holding a huge decanter. LAURA is carrying an expensive gift bag.

LAURA: Arghhh!!!!

She grabs SARAH and hugs her. TOM and GEORGE stand by awkwardly.

LAURA: It is sooooo good to see you!! You look amazing. And look at all this! I really never thought…and you must be George?!!

GEORGE: That's me!

LAURA: I would say I've heard so much about you, but we haven't spoken for…god, it's been ages.

TOM: Sarah.

They hug.

TOM: This place is just gorgeous. Look at you, all settled down! You're a lucky *boy* George.

GEORGE: I am.

SARAH: He is.

TOM: Wow. Look at all this space. It's amazing what you can get for your money out here.

SARAH: Yup. If you're willing to live a million miles from the action!

LAURA: No, it really is beautiful. I'm so happy for you!

SARAH: Just ignore the chaos, we ran out of time –

TOM: Big delivery?

GEORGE: Yup. Check this out. You put the gnocchi in here, and it griddles it for you.

TOM: Right.

SARAH: We only moved in two weeks ago, so you know…

TOM: Well with a bit of paint here and bit of paint there you'll soon feel at home.

GEORGE: We've actually painted this room.

LAURA: It looks fantastic. I love what you've done with this plant. It's such a bold statement.

GEORGE: Thanks Laura, I thought so to.

TOM: Here. For you. House warming.

SARAH: Thanks, you shouldn't have…

GEORGE: It's really lovely.

TOM: Decanter. Receipt is included. Should you hate it.

GEORGE: Oh, no, we don't.

SARAH: It will go very well with the plant.

LAURA: So what's it like around here then?

SARAH: Well it's not Islington.

LAURA: No, but Islington wasn't Islington ten years ago.

TOM: Yes it was.

LAURA: Oh you know what I mean.

SARAH: Well one day at a time, there was a stabbing in the park last week. Helicopters and everything.

LAURA: Oh wow.

SARAH: Yup. And I'm surprised you weren't delayed getting here because it took me forever to get –

TOM: We got an Uber. Best way to travel when going off the grid.

SARAH: Yup. And we are way off it.

LAURA: Chin up, I read in the *Standard's* 'Home and Property' section last week that this is shaping up to be London's most desirable post-code. /

GEORGE: Yup.

LAURA: / So *you've* done *so* well to buy here.

TOM: Very canny investment.

LAURA: Apparently it's going to be the new Dalston.

SARAH: Ha! Well tell that to the shop on the corner, and maybe they'll rethink their wine stock. It's Echo Falls all round tonight I'm afraid –

LAURA: No, wait…

LAURA hands over a very expensive bottle of wine.

SARAH: Oh wow.

LAURA: I brought a little something for the table.

GEORGE: I've never tried this.

TOM: They do say you pay for good wine and this one is *really* good.

TOM makes himself at home on the sofa, and in doing so moves a cushion out of the way and inadvertently covers Arthur's box with it.

LAURA: Well I don't get to drink as much as I did in the old days, so when I do it's such a treat.

SARAH: How is Florrie?

LAURA: Who is Florrie?!

SARAH: Oh god, have I said the wrong – that is her name, yes?

LAURA: Yes, yes, I was joking, I meant –

TOM: She's fine, she's with Magda. Au pair. Not attractive. Bulgarian. Wouldn't let me get a Scando.

LAURA: Ignore him. Darling, I just don't want to talk about kids tonight. I want it to be like old times. If that's okay with you?

SARAH: Perfect.

LAURA: I've missed you.

SARAH: You too, both of you.

TOM: Whatever you've been doing to her George, it's been extremely positive.

GEORGE: … Thanks…

LAURA: You actually look seventeen months younger, rather than older. Not like me.

SARAH: No, you look –

TOM: It can't be helped darling, pregnancy speeds up the ageing process.

LAURA: Oh fuck off, Tom.

TOM: What?

LAURA: He knows full well what.

SARAH: You look great.

LAURA: Thank you. See, Tom, it's as simple as that. Seventeen months.

SARAH: Has it really been that long?

LAURA: It was Florrie's second birthday.

SARAH: Blink and it's gone.

LAURA: Yes. Sarah was the only childless adult there, lucky thing, so she drank *all* the wine, insisted on taking over the iPod for musical chairs and tried to turn the whole thing into a rave.

GEORGE: Really? That doesn't sound like Sarah.

LAURA: And then... Oh my god...and then, she tried to get all the other parents to go out with her to some bar afterwards.

SARAH: Yup.

LAURA: I think you even...

SARAH: Don't –

LAURA: She came back later, a total mess, and cried on the sofa for over an hour!!

SARAH: Yes, well it was...

LAURA: Oh, sorry. I shouldn't have said that, should I? I didn't mean...

LAURA goes to sit on the sofa, where the cushion is placed.

GEORGE: No, wait!!

GEORGE grabs the box.

SARAH: That's Arthur.

GEORGE: He's my tortoise. I'll just put him somewhere safe.

GEORGE puts him on the kitchen counter, then begins to open, pour and pass the wine.

LAURA: Tortoise? Really? Oh that is so cute!!! Can I see him?

GEORGE: He's hibernating.

SARAH: You can't wake them up when they're hibernating or they die. George has been really worried about him /

GEORGE: Well it's been so hot he'll be ever so confused.

SARAH: / because the heat can wake them up early.

TOM: How interesting.

SARAH: George has had him since he was six.

LAURA: Oh my god, adorable.

Awkward silence. GEORGE hands SARAH her glass.

LAURA: I've missed you so much! I'm so glad that we're finally back in a room together.

SARAH: Oh thank George for tonight. I had no idea you were coming.

LAURA: Oh?

TOM: Really?

LAURA: But you said –

SARAH: Actually, it wasn't me who messaged you. It was George. On my account.

GEORGE: I did take matters into my own hands somewhat.

LAURA: You *fraped* her?!

SARAH: Yes, and I'm so glad he did. This is a lovely surprise.

TOM: Cheers.

ALL: Cheers!!

C1.

They are gathered round the table. Drinks have been drunk. GEORGE is dishing out food.

TOM: So how did you two meet?

SARAH: Oh well that's a really, really long story.

GEORGE: It's not that long.

SARAH: It is –

GEORGE: Tinder.

LAURA: What, the sex thing!?

GEORGE: Yep. The sex thing.

SARAH: I tindered him after a really shit date.

LAURA: What?

GEORGE: Yep, she'd been on a date with Wet Frank.

SARAH: That's our name for him: Wet Frank, there was more of his artisan beer in his beard than he actually drank. And I mean have you ever kissed a wet beard?

LAURA: Disgusting.

SARAH: Yeah, totally, but by the time he'd finally stopped wanking on about farmers markets, what feminism means to him and his highly unoriginal plans to start his own microbrewery, I'd missed the overground. So I thought I'd just go back to his. I mean, we'd come this far, so I thought I should at least give it a go. And I'd given everything downstairs a tidy up, nice underwear, I can't waste it.

GEORGE: That's my girl.

By now, GEORGE is clearing away some of the plates and dishes ready for desert. During the following he rinses some plates, stacks the dishwasher, etc.

SARAH: But anyway, we get back to his, and I'm there on top of the guy, like, riding him, and he's still going on and on. About how much he likes me, and how he thinks we shouldn't have sex yet, he thinks I've had too much to drink –

LAURA: You always have too much to drink.

SARAH: Thank you Laura. Well I bloody needed to to get in the mood for him. But now it's backfired because he doesn't want to take advantage of me. I mean, for fuck's sake! This is *Tinder*, not *Guardian Soulmates*.

TOM: So what did you do?

SARAH: I just got up, got dressed and left.

LAURA: Yes!!

SARAH: Yep. Because sometimes you have to realize you've made a horrible mistake, and just walk away.

LAURA: Hear hear.

TOM: Don't you go getting ideas Laura!!

SARAH: But by this time I need sex. So I've opened up Tinder and set it to a mile radius.

TOM: Who swiped right first?

LAURA: Swiped right?

SARAH: It's a Tinder thing...

TOM: To get a match, you have to both swipe right on each other's photos –

LAURA: How do you know how Tinder works?

TOM: Everyone knows.

LAURA: I don't.

TOM: ... A colleague showed me.

LAURA: Which colleague?

TOM: ... John. If I was to guess, I would assume Sarah swiped right first.

SARAH: Yeah, yeah I did actually, not that it's a crime.

TOM: That's not what I was inferring.

LAURA: That's who you are. Proactive.

GEORGE: Basically, I was the first to respond.

SARAH: Yep.

GEORGE: First come, first served.

SARAH: Alright, I'm not a Harvester's buffet. You were also funny. I asked him what he was doing and he said he was watching *Ice Road Truckers*, on repeat.

GEORGE: It wasn't a joke. I actually was.

SARAH: So I turn up. And we have a few drinks, not that I need any more... We laugh. And then... I pass out on his sofa.

GEORGE: Yep. Out cold.

SARAH: And then the next morning I wake up with a blanket over me, still wearing all my underwear, so I know he's not a creep, and we end up having breakfast, and breakfast becomes lunch, and lunch becomes drinks and drinks becomes –

GEORGE: Good times.

SARAH: Yeah, good times.

LAURA: You haven't changed.

SARAH: I'm going to take that as a compliment.

LAURA: Of course. So modern.

GEORGE: Yep. And here we are now. Cohabiters. Owners.

TOM: Here's to Wet Frank.

ALL: To Wet Frank!

LAURA: And so what next?

SARAH: Next?

LAURA: Children?!

TOM: Sarah the Mother.

SARAH: Who knows.

GEORGE: We'll see.

TOM: You've got the space.

SARAH pours more wine.

LAURA: You'll have to cut back on the wine.

She continues to pour.

LAURA: Clock is ticking. I know so many people who have left it too late.

GEORGE: How about you guys?

LAURA: Oh we are b-ding again.

TOM: She means fucking.

LAURA: Baby dancing, Tom!

SARAH: He meant, how did you meet.

TOM: Oh, how did we meet?

GEORGE: Yeah.

LAURA: Pass me the wine.

SARAH: Go on Tom, don't be shy, how did you two meet?

TOM: We met through Sarah.

SARAH: Yeah, I was cupid, but instead of a bow I used my vagina.

GEORGE: What?!

GEORGE, open mouthed, accidentally allows a set of cutlery to slide off the dirty plate he's holding.

GEORGE: Shit.

LAURA: *(To GEORGE.)* Here, let me help you.

LAURA picks up the cutlery and helps him clear up.

TOM: Sarah and I used to date.

LAURA: Unsuccessfully.

SARAH: Have you not put two and two together yet?

TOM: Not awkward is it?

GEORGE: Oh my god, is this Tom?

SARAH: Yes.

GEORGE: You're Tom. Brilliant.

TOM: Yes.

GEORGE: Brilliant.

TOM: Indeed! So I guess that makes us Eskimo brothers?

SARAH: Eskimo brothers?!

TOM: Yeah! Eskimo brothers. We've both shared the same igloo.

LAURA: Oh my god, Tom!

GEORGE: I've never heard anyone actually say that out loud before.

SARAH: Can we not? Talk about this? Please?

TOM: Sorry.

LAURA goes to put a heavy serving dish down on the kitchen side, right where Arthur's box is.

GEORGE: Wait!!

GEORGE grabs the box.

LAURA: Oh my god, is that –

GEORGE: Arthur?

SARAH: Yup.

LAURA: I am SO sorry.

GEORGE: No harm done, I'll just put him somewhere safe.

GEORGE returns Arthur to the sofa.

LAURA: I'm so pleased you've finally met someone. It's so exciting. And going forward what ever you decide about starting a family is –

GEORGE: We've not really talked about it.

LAURA: Really?

SARAH: Moving on.

TOM: No more baby talk, we hear you.

SARAH: Look just because you decided to give up your life as it was –

LAURA: Things change Sarah. For better or worse. I just hope you realize that either way you're currently making a decision. Doing nothing is making a decision.

GEORGE: I'm up for it.

SARAH: George!

GEORGE: I love the sound of a baby dance.

SARAH: And that's why we haven't talked about having children.

GEORGE: I actually do do a dance as part of our foreplay. Pretty sexy.

SARAH: Seriously, give it a rest.

GEORGE: I'm kidding. You know I'll go along with anything you want, right? We can carry on as we are, or we can change everything. Whatever makes you happy makes me happy.

SARAH: We haven't even had a chance to talk about my work let alone having children.

GEORGE: What do you mean?

SARAH: It's okay, forget about it.

GEORGE: No, no what's going on?

SARAH: Actually now's probably not the right time. Let's talk about it later?

LAURA: We don't mind.

SARAH: It's fine.

LAURA: Clearly everything is not fine.

SARAH: It's just work.

TOM: You've not been deemed surplus to requirement?

LAURA: Oh God, you've not been let go!?

SARAH: No! No, I've not been let go. If you must know, they've offered me a partnership.

LAURA: Congratulations!

GEORGE: Really?

SARAH: Yeah, really.

LAURA: Oh my god! Let's raise a glass to your achievement!

SARAH: Well, maybe don't raise a glass just yet. I haven't –

TOM: No we must, this is top draw! Promotion is the holy grail. Equals more money. Equals –

SARAH: Longer hours, less time here, more crap to deal with, more pressure, more, more, more everything becomes about more. More of the same…

TOM: Exactly!

LAURA: I can already picture how you're going to transform this room! SARAH: I just don't know if it's the right time for me.

TOM: Is there ever a wrong time for more money?! No.

LAURA: I can't pretend I'm not a little bit jealous.

SARAH: There's cheese to come, Tom.

TOM: Cheese! Oh, that is music to my ears.

LAURA: No Tom, you know you can't have cheese – it goes straight through him.

GEORGE: Don't you want to talk about this?

SARAH: Later George, let's talk about this later.

D1.

Desert plates sit half empty on the table and coffee and wine are being poured and drunk. TOM is eating cheese.

LAURA: I suppose one problem could help solve the other. This whole situation will make you look at the future in a different light.

TOM: Laura –

LAURA: I'm trying to help.

TOM: I know, but perhaps tread carefully –

LAURA: No, I'm sorry Tom, but this is important. I fought my natural instincts for so long. I didn't want anything to get in the way of a good night out or my career /

SARAH: Can we not do this.

LAURA: / but then I met Tom, and I just couldn't fight it any more. And it was the best decision I ever made.

SARAH: Was it? Really?

LAURA: What do you mean?

SARAH: It's just that the road you've taken just looks a lot like the road where you kiss goodbye to ever having fun ever again.

GEORGE: Sarah…

SARAH: It looks like the road where you're so lonely that you spend those rare moments with friends trying to persuade them all to have kids too, so you'll be less miserable.

LAURA: That's not true.

SARAH: I'm sorry. Sorry. I didn't mean that. It's just that's not what this is about, Laura. It's not about having kids, or not having kids. I just feel like I'm at a fucking huge fork in the road. I can't even decide what to do with my own life right now, let alone look after someone else.

GEORGE: Sarah, what's –

LAURA: Forever dramatic.

SARAH: I beg your pardon?

LAURA: Darling, to listen to you you'd think the world is ending. Take stock. You have a…lovely home. I mean who would have thought all those years ago, that you'd settle down, but you've found the loveliest young man. And now the offer of your dream job. Yet you still have to add drama. You've worked your whole life for this.

SARAH: And perhaps that is the tragedy.

TOM: Tragedy is not a six figure pay package I can tell you that.

SARAH: Really?

LAURA: Well if you're not starting a family, you should at least be following the money.

TOM: Trust me, it's a wonderful club to be part of.

SARAH: Why, so I can buy a bigger car, or more crap to fill –

TOM: A house in Islington!

SARAH: Fuck Islington.

LAURA: You do not mean that.

SARAH: I don't want to be ransomed to a job just so I can live surrounded by organic grocers and fancy coffee shops.

TOM: You like organic grocers.

SARAH: Yes, but –

GEORGE: I thought you loved your job.

SARAH: I did. I do. I just don't know if it's want I want to do forever…

LAURA: Sarah, this is not like you at all! You ARE your job.

SARAH: But, but – I don't know if that's who I want to be any more. I mean, I've spent all these years, hours upon hours, days, weekends, essentially doing nothing.

GEORGE: That is not true. You work harder than anyone else I know.

SARAH: I have spent thousands of hours managing an account in which a CGI Hippo hula dances in order to sell a biscuit. A biscuit! Two-hundred solid days for a fucking biscuit! My life is a fucking joke.

GEORGE: Heh, heh, people love biscuits and hippo's and hula dancing, and you combined them – you saw that heavenly combo.

SARAH: Is that really the best I can do in life? Think about what animal I can pair up with some piece of crap to make people want to buy more stuff that they don't really need, that will make them fat, or give them liver failure or just end up in landfill in six months. Is that really the best I can do?

LAURA: That's not true, Sarah.

SARAH: It is, it really is. Everyday we go to work and make the world a shittier place.

GEORGE: Hmmmm…

SARAH: Everyone except you then, George.

LAURA: You're into the obnoxious stage of drunkenness, I see.

SARAH: Well at least I've got the drink as an excuse.

LAURA: Are you just going to sit there eating cheese?

TOM: What do you want me to do? Tell her she's having a crisis? Why bother? It's nothing new, she's always having a crisis. Today it's about her role in the world. Tomorrow it will be about her teeth, or feminism, or socialism, or some other ism. The day after it will be about not having babies. But it won't actually change anything.

GEORGE: Now that is unnecessary.

TOM: You seem like a really sweet guy, George.

GEORGE: At least put the brie down if you're going to insult me.

TOM: Sweet is not an insult. Naive, even that's not an insult. It's just who you are: a very sweet young guy.

GEORGE: And you're a bed shitter.

TOM: What?

SARAH: George…

GEORGE: Yeah, she told me.

SARAH: Oh god…

SARAH moves away to the sofa, moving Arthur onto the floor as she sits.

GEORGE: Yeah. I mean no wonder she broke it off. That's pretty disgusting. Great story though!

TOM: Is that what she told you?

SARAH: Of course I told him, it's hard to forget a fountain of shit spraying onto my leg!

LAURA: It's a medical condition!

SARAH: Is it, really?

GEORGE: Don't worry, we all get caught short sometimes.

TOM: Thank you.

LAURA: This isn't funny, we've already lost one cleaner because of this!! God, Sarah, is that why you're giving him cheese now?!

SARAH: Possibly subconsciously...

LAURA: That's such awful hosting, we have Egyptian cotton sheets. Tom, stop eating cheese!!

TOM finally does.

LAURA: Did I hurt you that much?

SARAH: What?

LAURA: I'm sorry, okay. I'm sorry that you two broke up and I'm sorry Tom and I are together /

SARAH: It's a bit late for that now.

LAURA: / and I'm sorry I moved out –

SARAH: Laura, I don't give a shit about you or Tom or you moving out.

LAURA: Clearly you do.

SARAH: No, it's the best thing that ever happened to me. Aside from you George.

GEORGE: I can see why I'd come second to that.

SARAH: You made me so sad and so vain and fundamentally empty. With your shitty Egyptian cotton sheets. Pathetic.

LAURA: Egyptian cotton sheets have never been pathetic. Never!

SARAH: Listen to yourself!

LAURA: A decade later and you're still the same as you were in your twenties. Now that's pathetic.

SARAH: Is it? Just because I haven't followed your lame path of getting married, having children… It doesn't make me a loser. And perhaps George is naive /

GEORGE: Sarah?

SARAH: / but at least he operates in the real world. What you do actually means something.

LAURA: Oh yes, the noble art of teaching.

SARAH: Oh come on. Your job is totally pointless.

LAURA: I'm sorry?

SARAH: I mean, come on, PR. Public Relations. For toilet roll! What does that even mean? Just, who CARES?!

LAURA: Are you telling me we don't need toilet paper? Telling me people don't need to wipe their arse?! Because I think people should wipe their arse!!

SARAH: Well there's your tombstone written right there. And Tom, your job's just cruel, isn't it? it's…like really you're morally a Dolphin Fucker.

TOM: That's a new one to me.

SARAH: Come on, you know J. P. Morgan are basically Mordor.

TOM: Completely, everyday I just sit there in my evil office plotting the world's destruction.

SARAH: This isn't a joke.

TOM: I think you have a warped view of the financial sector, closest I get to fucking a dolphin is eating a tuna sandwich from Marks and Spencer's.

SARAH: I don't think I do. I think I know exactly what it is. And I think, if you did stop and think about what you do everyday, then I don't think you'd be able to carry on. I think you'd just grind to a halt. I think that –

TOM: All I'm hearing is the word think.

SARAH: Don't take the piss. I'm trying to make sense of this.

TOM: Is that what you're doing?

SARAH: Stop interrupting me, I can't –

TOM: Think?

SARAH: Yes, I can't think with all the interruptions.

TOM: But you can certainly say it.

SARAH: This is my whole adult life, everything I've worked for, wanted and it's been a waste.

LAURA: She's on a journey, Tom.

SARAH: Yes, maybe I am on a journey, maybe that is the wanky term you can apply to this moment right now. /

TOM: God, well I hope this is better than that film *Eat Pray Love* you made me endure.

SARAH: / Are you not scared that your huge car, and your massive house, and all that expensive, and to be pretty honest, utterly bland furniture you fill it with.

LAURA: Take that back, we have exceptional taste!

SARAH: Come on, look at that fucking disgusting decanter, how much did that cost, a week's wages?!

TOM: Maybe for certain people.

SARAH: All of it, everything, they're just great distractions, aren't they?

TOM: You've obviously never driven an A5.

SARAH: Ahhh!

GEORGE: Shall we call it a night?

SARAH: Don't go yet.

LAURA: We're not going out onto that street, unless there's an Uber right outside the door!

SARAH: No, George, you wanted to talk about it, so let's do this.

GEORGE: Okay. Okay.

SARAH: All of those things they make it all seem worth it for you, don't they.

TOM: I have no idea what is rhetorical or just plain old noise here.

SARAH: I know you need to convince yourself that all this money and stuff is what matters, because otherwise the truth will hit you that your job is at best pointless and at worst fucking destructive.

LAURA: You're angry with us because of our money.

SARAH: I know you might find this hard to understand Laura but not everything is about money.

TOM: Why destructive?

SARAH: You know full well why.

TOM: Tell me.

GEORGE: How close is your Uber?

TOM: What do you want to say, Sarah? The money I earn is evil? Okay, take my tax out, there goes George's wage. One less teacher.

SARAH: That's the only way you see the world isn't it: as a transaction.

TOM: I'm really bored of you now.

SARAH: So you're not going to discuss this?

TOM: Not with someone who has nothing new or intelligent to say, no. Is our Uber on the way?

LAURA: Of course not, we're in the middle of bloody nowhere!

SARAH: Fuck off!

SARAH heads to the kitchen area and begins clearing up.

SARAH: We should clear up this mess.

GEORGE: It can wait. You're right. This probably wasn't the best time to have this conversation...

SARAH: Actually, it was the perfect time to have this conversation. And do you know what – I've made a decision.

TOM: Oh here we go...

SARAH: Having these two vacuous shit-birds here has been a brilliant reminder of everything I don't want my life to be. So I'm going to say no. I don't want it.

TOM sarcastically slow claps.

GEORGE: Okay. That's enough now. Uber or not you're going out there with the '*gangs*'.

GEORGE moves over to help SARAH clear up.

LAURA: Sarah, you'll always be the same: hot air. All this talking, yet you'll probably take the job anyway. But you're right, you shouldn't have a child. You'd just fuck them up.

SARAH, who was in the process of clearing the table, is holding a half full glass of wine.

SARAH: Fuck you.

She throws the glass of wine in LAURA's face. It hits her and also splatters up the white wall behind her.

SARAH: Get out.

Silence. Then the beep of a phone.

TOM: The end is here. Let's go.

SARAH and GEORGE are rather forcefully and aggressively clearing up, and ignoring their guests.

TOM takes LAURA's arm and leads her towards the door. As he does he accidentally treads on the box that contains Arthur. A crack. TOM freezes. Neither SARAH or GEORGE have noticed. LAURA looks on in horror. TOM straightens out the box and places it back on the sofa. SARAH turns just as he does so, have they just been caught? It appears not.

SARAH: What are you waiting for?! Out!

LAURA: This. Us. Everything. Is over.

SARAH: Finally!

TOM picks up the decanter and makes to leave.

SARAH: Oi dolphin fucker, you can't take a gift.

TOM: Thought it was disgusting.

SARAH: It is.

They have hold of it together. They stare at each other. They both let go of it. It smashes. TOM and LAURA exit.

E1.

SARAH is staring at the broken decanter. GEORGE returns from seeing TOM and LAURA out.

SARAH: Gone?

GEORGE: Gone. There's no turning back now.

SARAH: End of something beautiful. Not that it was ever beautiful.

GEORGE: You were right: proper arseholes.

SARAH: I lost control.

GEORGE: I've never seen anything like it.

SARAH: I shouldn't have called them shit-birds.

GEORGE: I don't know…seemed pretty apt.

SARAH: Can we just start this evening again?

GEORGE: It's a bit late for that now. I wish we'd talked about all this sooner.

SARAH: Well, it was a bit difficult, wasn't it?

GEORGE: If I'd known what you were feeling. If you'd spoken to me I wouldn't have invited them. It seemed like such a good idea at the time. Remind me never to invite your friends over again.

SARAH: Okay.

GEORGE: Vacuous shit-birds.

SARAH: What did they say?

GEORGE: Out there? Nothing. Stood there in silence. Waiting to be taken away. I couldn't work out if they were shocked or just pissed off. Who knows, perhaps they're used to people telling them that their whole lives are meaningless.

SARAH: I doubt it, they only hear what they want to hear.

GEORGE: Are you feeling better?

SARAH: They're gone, so yes.

GEORGE: I don't mean that.

SARAH: Should I want to feel better? Isn't this just a perfectly normal reaction to the state of things?

GEORGE: What things?

SARAH: Things. Everything.

GEORGE: The price of Echo Falls?

SARAH: I know you're trying to make me feel better but now's not the time.

GEORGE: Sorry.

SARAH: I just…every time I open my eyes there's another shit storm kicking off somewhere, and when I try to think about what I might do to try to make things better, I don't – I can only see wrong choices. Things that will make everything worse. Ways to fuck up our already fucked up world.

GEORGE: How long have you felt like this?

SARAH: I don't know. A while.

GEORGE: Sarah, I'm not going to tell you how to think, but if I can just say what I think is this: there is something beautiful about not letting things in.

SARAH: But it's everywhere. There's so much wrong that I can't not see it. There's no way of not knowing anymore.

GEORGE: There is. I know that all that stuff is out there. I see it in my newsfeed, on the front page of a paper in the shop, but I just keep it out there. I don't let it in.

SARAH: Right.

GEORGE: Because what difference does it make, really? If I worry about things I can't change? Start picking holes, all you'll see is darkness. Jeez, that sounded much heavier than I meant. You get what I mean though, right?

SARAH: I think so.

GEORGE goes and picks up Arthur.

GEORGE: Just think. In a couple of months, Arthur will wake up. Like he has every year for the past twenty. And he will keep doing that every year for another fifty years. I find that extraordinarily comforting.

A nod. GEORGE puts Arthur down on the table. They stare at the decanter.

GEORGE: What do you want to do with this?

SARAH: I don't know. Ignore it. For now.

She goes and tops up her wine.

They wait.
It appears to be over.
They go to bow.
Then…suddenly music.

SARAH is initially confused but then she see's that everyone else is starting to set up – so she follows suit.

RESET.

GEORGE, SARAH, TOM and LAURA reset. They try to clean and remove the plates, food and rubbish. They try to clean the wine stain off the white wall but it just damages the set, revealing some of the rubbish they've just hidden. There's just not time to clean everything up, so they simply take everything off, piling it at each side, then bring on new items to replace them: new plates are set, a new ikea bag, a new box preset off for the package, and new bags of food. They retire to their starting positions.

A – simply indicates that it's SARAH's turn to speak but she can't find the words.

A2.

GEORGE and SARAH's living room. East London. They have only recently moved in. To the audience, the space is a mess, but the company continue as though it were a soon to be stylish sitting room.

But… SARAH isn't ready yet. She can't find the Echo Falls in all the mess, and there's a mark on her shirt she can't get off. She's also struggling to get her shoes and coat back on for her entrance, which has caught her unawares.

SARAH: Sorry sorry sorry, I know I'm late!!

SARAH enters, flustered. She has a shopping bag with her. The actor puts the bag down by the front door, the wrong place.

GEORGE: They'll be here in fifteen minutes.

SARAH: I'm sorry.

GEORGE: What happened?

SARAH: What happened is that it is time to turn round and go back…(?)

SARAH is momentarily thrown by what she said. GEORGE continues as normal, rummaging and finally finding some plates and unpacking them onto the kitchen counter.

GEORGE: Right.

SARAH: Seriously, it's complete fucking chaos out there. And as if it isn't bad enough on a normal day, tonight the just tube just decides to stop dead /

GEORGE: Uh huh.

SARAH: Are you even listening to me?

GEORGE: Yes. Yup. Definitely. Did you get the wine?

SARAH: I didn't have enough time to get to Waitrose. So I had to go to the shop on the corner, which only stocks Echo Falls.

GEORGE: Oh well.

SARAH: Oh well? That is not the correct response to a full-blown crisis.

GEORGE: It's just wine.

SARAH: Seriously, this is a massive fucking crisis.

GEORGE: Calm down!

SARAH: I will not calm down! I don't know what's going on.

GEORGE: You poor, poor thing.

SARAH: They made no announcements. Not one! There's just too many people. There's no space. The temperature, is getting obscene. I mean, it's *so hot.*

GEORGE: Which is why I'm so worried about Arthur.

SARAH: It's a fucking mess. What have you been doing all day?

GEORGE: I've had a very busy day as it happens!

SARAH clocks the Ikea bag.

SARAH: So I see.

GEORGE waits for SARAH to pull out a kitchen implement, she doesn't – so he does.

GEORGE: I spent all morning trying to find the cutlery and roasting tins, and then I decided it would be quicker to just pop out and buy some more.

SARAH: Every box is labeled.

GEORGE: There's no mention of roasting tins on any boxes.

SARAH: Jesus Christ, they're in the box marked glasses – no, kitchen equipment!

GEORGE: I got a garlic press.

SARAH: –

GEORGE: You know what it's like…you get to the bit past the show room, you know, where they keep all the funky stuff…

SARAH: –

GEORGE: The Marketplace. And somehow, before you know it, you end up with a trolley full of really cool stuff.

This time GEORGE puts the apron on himself.

SARAH: Mmmm. Really cool.

GEORGE: So I have had a very productive day thank you. And now it's wine o'clock, Echo Falls or not.

He pulls out a pack of wine glasses.

SARAH: We have wine glasses already!!

GEORGE: Yes, but not unpacked. I couldn't find them either. And these were four pounds. FOUR POUNDS!!

Pointing at a box.

GEORGE: So you don't want a glass then.

SARAH: Yes. Fine. Why not. But it's warm because they don't keep it in the fridge.

GEORGE: Oh wait. No. Wait until you see this!! Finally arrived, from Japan, I'll have you know.

GEORGE opens the freezer compartment, water comes flooding out. A moment. He ignores it and pulls out an ice cube tray which contains only water. Meanwhile, SARAH steps out of the way of the water that has come pouring from the freezer, she can't help but stare at it.

Ta da! This should do the trick. Look. I told you I'd had a productive day.

SARAH stares at GEORGE in disbelief as he pours the water into a glass and continues oblivious to the surrounding mess.

SARAH: I really need to talk…

GEORGE: Arthur!! There you are you naughty boy.

SARAH belatedly pops the cork as GEORGE picks up a small brown box, which was on the chair. He listens, then says very quietly.

I think he's okay.

SARAH: George!

GEORGE: Alright. I'll just pop him somewhere safe.

SARAH: Don't go when I'm trying to tell you something.

He places the box on the sofa.

GEORGE: Yes sorry, you were saying. A productive day.

SARAH: The reason I was late –

The smoke alarm begins to go off.

GEORGE: Shit shit shit!!

He runs to the oven and pulls out a casserole.

Phew. Caught it.

However this time there is more smoke than before. GEORGE remains oblivious and continues to wave packing in front of the smoke alarm until it stops.

Sorry. What were you saying about the reason you were late?

GEORGE continues to lay the table.

SARAH: George, I. I had a meeting and something came up which meant we had to go to the pub –

GEORGE: Say no more.

SARAH: But I –

GEORGE: No, I get it. Part and parcel of the job.

GEORGE has now disappeared off into the hall. But there is no plant pre-set. LAURA subtly appears at the other side of the stage and places the plant from the first repetition on the edge of the set.

SARAH: No listen, it was…

GEORGE heads across and takes the pot that LAURA had left. GEORGE places it on the table.

What the *hell?*

GEORGE: It's a plant. I told you I'd had a productive –

SARAH: It's not a plant, it's a hedge you're putting a hedge on our dinner table.

GEORGE: I like it.

SARAH: Well you seem to like living here /

GEORGE: Yes, I do.

SARAH: / so your opinion is clearly warped.

Pause.

Tell me it's going to be okay.

GEORGE: It's going to be okay.

SARAH: I just didn't think this is where we'd end up.

GEORGE: I know. But isn't that amazing, we're on a true adventure, not knowing what the future has in store.

SARAH stares at the water that is spreading around her. GEORGE kisses SARAH.

SARAH: Speaking of our future though –

Doorbell.

I'm not ready.

GEORGE: It'll be okay.

SARAH: This is a mess!

GEORGE: Well we can't do anything about it now, can we?

GEORGE exits. SARAH touches the water that is on the floor: yes, it is real. GEORGE returns with a box, a skip in his step, albeit the actor now has to be careful about slipping.

GEORGE: Carry on, as you were. It's not them.

SARAH: I can see that. What is it?

GEORGE: I don't know. The TV? The microwave? That record player you ordered from eBay.

They open the box. It's full of packaging.

SARAH: Hurry up!

GEORGE: Okay.

SARAH: We don't have time –

GEORGE: Fantastic!!

GEORGE pulls out a fishing net full of plastic and dead sea animals.

SARAH: What the hell?

GEORGE is stuck holding a fishing net.

GEORGE: A…gnocchi griddle…

SARAH: You've got to be joking?

GEORGE has subtly covered this change by putting the fish back in the box.

GEORGE: …you just put the gnocchi here, push it down, and it griddles it for you.

SARAH: We do not need this.

GEORGE: Well that's what you think now, but this is going to change your gnocchi forev –

SARAH: Ah! You're just enabling the end of civilization.

GEORGE: Darling, you've probably got time to get changed now.

SARAH: –

GEORGE: You look great.

SARAH: –

GEORGE: But you know, it's a special occasion, I've put my shirt on.

SARAH: Yes you have.

GEORGE: And this is a very very special occasion.

SARAH: In what way?

GEORGE: Well… I've not actually invited Adele and Paul round.

SARAH: What's going on?

GEORGE: "OMG It's been so long. I miss you so much. Completely. We must rectify this. Yeah, that is an amazing idea."

SARAH: ?

GEORGE: Does that not feel familiar? They're your words.

SARAH: My words?

GEORGE: Verbatim. On Facebook. To Laura.

SARAH: Laura? …do not say Laura Rainsford.

GEORGE: Yep, the one and only. Surprise!

SARAH: I'm not sure what's happening.

GEORGE: *Sarah*, I'm telling you that Laura Rainsford is coming for dinner.

SARAH: –

GEORGE: And Tom.

SARAH: And fucking Tom!

GEORGE: You're making this sound less positive than I imagined.

SARAH: We need to stop this now.

GEORGE: It's too late.

SARAH: It's never too late.

GEORGE: Actually, this time it is.

SARAH: This is my worst nightmare.

Doorbell rings.

B2.

As TOM enters, he trips over SARAH's bag and drops the decanter. Everyone freezes but GEORGE expertly sweeps it away, grabs the third one from the props table and hands it to TOM.

LAURA is still covered in wine from the end of D1.

SARAH and GEORGE greet TOM and LAURA. TOM is now holding a huge decanter again. LAURA is carrying an expensive gift bag.

LAURA: Arghhh!!!!

LAURA grabs SARAH and hugs her. TOM and GEORGE stand by awkwardly.

It is sooooo good to see you!! You look amazing…
and you must be George?!!

GEORGE: That's me!

LAURA: I would say I've heard so much about you, but we haven't spoken for…god, it's been ages.

TOM: Sarah.

They hug.

This place is just gorgeous.

SARAH: We ran out of time – just ignore the chaos.

TOM: Well with a bit of paint here and bit of paint there you'll soon feel at home.

GEORGE: We've actually painted this room.

LAURA: It looks fantastic. I love what you've done with this plant. It's such a bold statement.

GEORGE: Thanks Laura, I thought so to.

TOM: House warming.

SARAH: You shouldn't have…

TOM: Decanter. Receipt is included, should you hate it.

GEORGE: Oh, no, we don't.

SARAH: You weren't delayed getting here?

TOM: We got an Uber. Best way to travel when going off the grid.

LAURA: Chin up, I read in the *Standard's* 'Home and Property' section last week that this is shaping up to be London's most desirable post-code. /

GEORGE: Yup.

LAURA: / So *you've* done *so* well to buy here.

TOM: Very canny investment.

LAURA: Apparently it's going to be the new Dalston.

SARAH: –

GEORGE: Ha! Well tell that to the shop on the corner, *eh Sarah*, and maybe they'll rethink their wine stock. /

SARAH: It's Echo Falls all round tonight I'm afraid –

GEORGE: / It's Echo Falls all round tonight I'm afraid –

LAURA: No, wait…

LAURA hands over a very expensive bottle of wine.

SARAH notices that water has begun to drip through the ceiling, off their stylish light fixture and onto the floor/table.

SARAH: Oh wow.

LAURA: I brought a little something for the table.

GEORGE: I've never tried this.

TOM: They do say you pay for good wine and this one is *really* good.

TOM makes himself at home on the sofa, and in doing so moves a cushion out of the way and inadvertently covers Arthur's box with it.

LAURA: Well I don't get to drink as much as I did in the old days, so when I do it's such a treat.

SARAH: –

SARAH watches the water drip from the light fixture. LAURA covers for her by skipping to the next section that she can start.

LAURA: I want it to be like old times. If that's okay with you?

SARAH: Perfect.

LAURA: I've missed you.

SARAH: You too, both of you.

TOM: Whatever you've been doing to her George, it's been extremely positive.

GEORGE: … Thanks…

LAURA: You actually look seventeen months younger, rather than older. Not like me.

SARAH subtly walks over to the edge of the stage to seek assurance from the stage manager.

GEORGE: No, you look –

TOM: It can't be helped darling, pregnancy speeds up the ageing process.

LAURA: Oh fuck off, Tom.

TOM: What?

LAURA: He knows full well what.

GEORGE: You look great.

LAURA: Thank you. See, Tom, it's as simple as that. Seventeen months.

SARAH returns, focused once more, having received a reassuring answer.

SARAH: Blink and it's gone.

LAURA: Yes. It was Florrie's second birthday. Sarah was the only childless adult there, lucky thing, so she drank *all* the wine, insisted on taking over the iPod for musical chairs and tried to turn the whole thing into a rave.

GEORGE: Really? That doesn't sound like Sarah.

LAURA: And then… Oh my god…and then, she tried to get all the other parents to go out with her to some bar afterwards.

SARAH: Don't –

LAURA: She came back later, a total mess, and cried on the sofa for over an hour!!

SARAH: Yes, well it was…

LAURA: Oh, sorry. I shouldn't have said that, should I? I didn't mean…

LAURA goes to sit on the sofa, where the cushion is placed.

GEORGE: No, wait!!

GEORGE grabs the box.

SARAH: That's Arthur.

GEORGE: He's my tortoise. I'll just put him somewhere safe.

GEORGE puts him on the kitchen counter, then begins to open, pour and pass the wine.

LAURA: Tortoise? Really? Oh that is so cute!!! Can I see him?

GEORGE: He's hibernating.

SARAH: You can't wake them up when they're hibernating or they die. /

GEORGE: Well it's been so hot he'll be ever so confused.

SARAH: / Because the heat can wake them up early.

TOM: How interesting.

LAURA: Oh my god, adorable.

Awkward silence. GEORGE hands SARAH her glass.

LAURA: I've missed you so much! I'm so glad that we're finally back in a room together.

SARAH: This is a surprise.

TOM: Cheers.

ALL: Cheers!!

Somehow, despite various obstacles, the actors manage to set up C2. SARAH is very conscious of the water still dripping from the light fitting. Because of this she is out of sync with the other actors as they sit.

C2.

Drinks have been drunk. GEORGE is dishing out food. The water is still dripping from the light fixture.

TOM: So how did you two meet?

SARAH: That's a really, really long story.

GEORGE: It's not that long.

SARAH: It is –

GEORGE: Tinder.

LAURA: What, the sex thing!?

GEORGE: Yep. The sex thing.

SARAH: A really shit date.

LAURA: What?

GEORGE: Yep, she'd been on a date with Wet Frank.

SARAH: Wet… Frank…

GEORGE: That's our name for him *isn't it*, Wet Frank.

SARAH: Yes.

GEORGE: As apparently there was more of his artisan beer in his beard than he actually drank, *wasn't there* Sarah?

SARAH: Yes.

GEORGE: And I mean have you ever kissed a wet beard?

SARAH: Yes.

LAURA: Disgusting.

SARAH: Yeah, totally.

TOM: So what did you do?

SARAH: I just got up, got dressed and left.

By now, GEORGE is clearing away some of the plates and dishes ready for desert. During the following he rinses some plates, stacks the dishwasher, etc.

LAURA: Yes!!

SARAH: Sometimes you have to realize you've made a horrible mistake, and just walk away.

LAURA: Hear hear.

TOM: Don't you go getting ideas Laura!!

SARAH: –

GEORGE: … And here we are now. Cohabiters. Owners.

TOM: Here's to Wet Frank.

ALL: To Wet Frank!

LAURA: … And so what next?

SARAH: Next?

LAURA: Children?!

TOM: Sarah the Mother.

SARAH: Who knows.

GEORGE: We'll see.

TOM: You've got the space.

SARAH pours more wine this time though the substance is oil. SARAH is shocked.

LAURA: You'll have to cut back on the wine.

This time though, SARAH doesn't pour anymore wine.

LAURA: Clock is ticking. I know so many people who have left it too late.

GEORGE: How about you guys?

LAURA: Oh we are b-ding again.

TOM: She means fucking.

LAURA: Baby dancing, Tom!

SARAH: –

GEORGE: I meant, how did you two meet?

TOM: Oh, how did we meet?

GEORGE: Yeah.

LAURA: Pass me the wine.

> *LAURA waits for SARAH to pass her the bottle as in the previous version. She doesn't. LAURA reaches over and takes it herself. SARAH tries to stop her but LAURA persists and gets the bottle. SARAH watches in horror as LAURA pours herself a glass of oil. She's now trying to carry on the action and stop LAURA from drinking.*

SARAH: Um, go on Tom, don't be shy, how did you two meet?

TOM: We met through Sarah.

SARAH: Yeah, I was cupid, but instead of a bow I used my vagina.

GEORGE: What?!

> *GEORGE, open mouthed, accidentally allows a set of cutlery to slide off the dirty plate he's holding.*

GEORGE: Shit.

LAURA: *(To GEORGE.)* Here, let me help you.

> *She picks up the cutlery and helps him clear up.*

TOM: Sarah and I used to date.

LAURA: Unsuccessfully.

> *SARAH snatches the oil filled glass from LAURA and almost misses her next line.*

SARAH: Have you not put two and two together yet?

TOM: Not awkward is it?

GEORGE: Oh my god, is this Tom?

SARAH: Yes.

GEORGE: You're Tom. Brilliant.

TOM: Yes.

GEORGE: Brilliant.

Bemused, LAURA takes the glass back and drinks. SARAH can't stop her. Slowly, imperceptibly, a sound begins to rise. It's not recognizable. Yet.

TOM: So I guess that makes us Eskimo brothers?

SARAH: Eskimo brothers?!

TOM: Yeah! Eskimo brothers. We've both shared the same igloo.

LAURA: Oh my god. Tom.

GEORGE: I've never heard anyone actually say that out loud before.

LAURA goes to put a heavy serving dish down on the kitchen side, right where Arthur's box is.

Wait!!

He grabs the box.

LAURA: Oh my god, is that –

GEORGE: Arthur?

SARAH: –

LAURA: I am SO sorry.

GEORGE: No harm done, I'll just put him somewhere safe.

He returns Arthur to the sofa.

LAURA: I'm so pleased you've finally met someone. It's so exciting. And going forward what ever you decide about starting a family is –

GEORGE: We've not really talked about it.

LAURA: Really?

SARAH: Moving on.

TOM: No more baby talk, we hear you.

The sound becomes more noticable now. It's unsettling. The others work harder to push the humour and energy over the top, but it seems to get under SARAH's skin. From the centre of the white table cloth, oil begins to spill. Just a tiny circle at first.

LAURA: Things change Sarah. For better or worse. I just hope you realize that either way you're currently making a decision. Doing nothing is making a decision.

GEORGE: I'm up for it.

SARAH: George!

GEORGE: I love the sound of a baby dance.

SARAH: –

GEORGE: I actually do do a dance as part of our foreplay. Pretty sexy.

SARAH: Give it a rest!

GEORGE: I'm kidding. You know I'll go along with anything you want, right? We can carry on as we are, or we can change everything. Whatever makes you happy makes me happy.

SARAH: We haven't even had a chance to talk about...

GEORGE: What do you mean?

SARAH: Forget about it.

GEORGE: No, no what's going on?

SARAH: Now's not the right time –

Sound sting. An oil drenched bird falls from the sky and lands by SARAH, she shrieks. Time stops and she stands and examines the object...

Shit!

She realizes what she's holding and drops the bird onto the floor. Time resumes.

LAURA: Are you okay?

SARAH: Yes.

Nobody else acknowledges what's happened. GEORGE attempts to restart the scene.

GEORGE: What's going on?

SARAH: It's fine.

LAURA: Clearly everything is not fine.

SARAH: …

TOM: You've not been deemed surplus to requirement?

LAURA: Oh God, you've not been let go!?

SARAH: No! No, they've offered me a…

LAURA: Congratulations!

GEORGE: Really?

SARAH: Yeah, really.

LAURA: Oh my god! Let's raise a glass to your achievement!

TOM: This is top draw! Promotion is the holy grail. Equals more money. Equals –

SARAH: More, more, more everything becomes about more.

TOM: Exactly!

TOM takes the bottle and pours them all an oily glass.

LAURA: I can already picture how you're going to transform this room!

Another bird lands by SARAH. This time she doesn't pick it up. She just stares at it. She realizes everyone is watching her.

I can't pretend I'm not a little bit jealous.

SARAH: Don't you want to talk about this?

GEORGE: It can wait, *Sarah*.

SARAH: There's cheese!!

TOM: Cheese! Oh, that is music to my ears.

LAURA: No Tom, you know you can't have cheese – it goes straight through him.

SARAH: We should clear up this mess.

They try to set up D2. The oil, water, rubbish, mean they occasionally stumble, struggle to complete it in time, but they still soldier on as though nothing were wrong.

D2.

Desert plates sit half empty on the table and coffee and wine are being poured and drunk. TOM is eating cheese. During the following scene, the oil on the table cloth will reach the edges of the table, run down and soak the sides of the cloth and begin to drip on the performers, covering them in oil. They are unsure of what's best: ignore it and get drenched, or move and risk acknowledging the problem. LAURA and TOM hold their ground, and GEORGE subtly maneuvers out of the way.

LAURA: This whole situation will make you look at the future in a different light.

TOM: Laura –

LAURA: No, Tom, this is important. I fought my natural instincts for so long and it was the best decision I ever made.

SARAH: Was it? Really?

LAURA: What do you mean?

SARAH: It's just that the road you've taken just looks a lot like the road where you kiss goodbye to life right now –

GEORGE: Sarah, what's –

LAURA: Forever dramatic.

SARAH: I beg your pardon?

LAURA: Darling, to listen to you you'd think the world is ending.

SARAH: And perhaps that is the tragedy.

TOM: Tragedy is not a six figure pay package I can tell you that.

SARAH: Really?

LAURA: Well if you're not starting a family, you should at least be following the money.

TOM: Trust me, it's a wonderful club to be part of.

SARAH: Why, so I can buy a bigger car, or more crap to fill –

TOM: A house in Islington!

SARAH: Fuck Islington.

Smoke has started to leak out from the oven.

GEORGE: I thought you loved your job.

The smoke from the oven is becoming more noticeable.

SARAH: Is this really the best I can do in life? Think about what animal I can make end up in landfill in six months. No, hang on…

LAURA: That's not true, Sarah.

SARAH: It is, it really is. Everyday we go to work and make the world a shittier place.

GEORGE: Hmmmm…

SARAH: Everyone.

LAURA: Are you just going to sit there eating cheese?

TOM: What do you want me to do? Tell her she's having a crisis? Why bother? It's nothing new, she's always having a crisis. Today it's about her role in the world. Tomorrow it will be about her teeth, or feminism, or socialism, or some other ism. The day after it will be about not having babies. But it won't actually change anything.

GEORGE: Now that is unnecessary.

TOM: You seem like a really sweet guy, George.

GEORGE: At least put the brie down if you're going to insult me.

TOM: Sweet is not an insult. Naive, even that's not an insult. It's just who you are: a very young man.

GEORGE: And you're a bed shitter.

TOM: What?

GEORGE: Yeah, she told me.

SARAH: . … Oh god…

SARAH is supposed to be moving Arthur onto the floor for the tortoise exit gag, but instead she's trying to stop the smoke pouring from the oven. She looks desperately into the wings for help.

GEORGE: Yeah. That's pretty disgusting.

TOM: Is that what she told you?

GEORGE: Of course Sarah told me, it was hard for her to forget a fountain of shit spraying onto her leg.

LAURA: It's a medical condition!

GEORGE: Is it, really?

SARAH exits briefly and is seen through the door holding a panicked conversation with a member of the crew about the smoke.

Don't worry, we all get caught short sometimes.

TOM: Thank you.

SARAH re-enters with a fire extinguisher which LAURA quickly snatches from her and hands back to a member of crew.

LAURA: This isn't funny, we've already lost one cleaner because of this!!

SARAH: …

LAURA: God, *Sarah.*

SARAH: …

LAURA: Awful hosting.

SARAH: …

LAURA: Tom, stop eating cheese!

TOM finally does.

I'm sorry, okay. I'm sorry /

SARAH: It's a bit late for that now.

LAURA: / I moved out –

Oil now pours down the fridge. It flows out of the sink. It's coming through the walls. Almost as though by the time they're finished, everything onstage will be black.

SARAH: I don't give a shit…

SARAH is now watching the oil. Pooling on the floor, it has started to move towards the sound cables downstage of their living room 'wall'.

LAURA: Clearly.

LAURA is exasperated by SARAH's refusal to engage with her.

GEORGE: …what about Laura's job, *Sarah?*

SARAH: –

GEORGE: I mean, come on, PR. Public Relations. For toilet roll! What does that even mean? Just, who CARES?!

LAURA: Are you telling me we don't need toilet paper? Telling me people don't need to wipe their arse?! Because I think people should wipe their arse!!

GEORGE: Well there's your tombstone written right there.
And Tom, Dolphin Fucker.

TOM: That's a new one to me.

GEORGE: Come on, you know J. P. Morgan are basically
Mordor.

TOM: Completely, everyday I just sit there in my evil office,
plotting the world's destruction.

SARAH: YES!

TOM: I think you have a warped view of the financial sector.

The smoke has now set off the fire alarm on set. We can barely hear.

SARAH: I don't think I do. I think I know exactly what it is.
And I think, if you did stop and think about what you do
everyday, then I don't think you'd be able to carry on.
I think you'd just grind to a halt. I think that –

TOM: All I'm hearing is the word think.

*SARAH becomes more and more disorientated as the noise builds.
She can't think straight. GEORGE tries to fan the alarm off but it
doesn't go.*

SARAH: Don't mock me. I'm trying to make sense of this.

TOM: Is that what you're doing?

SARAH: Stop interrupting me, I can't –

TOM: Think?

SARAH: Yes, I can't think with all the interruptions.

TOM: But you can certainly say it.

SARAH: This is my whole adult life, everything I've worked
for, wanted and it's been a waste.

LAURA: She's on a journey, Tom.

SARAH: –

TOM: God, well I hope this is better than that film *Eat Pray Love* you made me endure.

Another bird falls from the sky.

SARAH: Are you not scared –

TOM: You've obviously never driven an A5.

SARAH: Ahhh!

Now the theatre's alarm system is going off. The noise is excruciating.

GEORGE: Shall we call it a night.

SARAH: Yes!

TOM: I have no idea what is rhetorical or just plain old noise here.

LAURA: You're angry with us because of our money.

SARAH: Not everything is about money. This is pointless and fucking destructive.

TOM: Why destructive?

SARAH: …

TOM: Tell me.

GEORGE: How close is your Uber?

TOM: What do you want to say, Sarah? /

SARAH: Stop, that's what I want you to say: stop, stop, STOP!

TOM: / The money I earn is evil? Okay, take my tax out, there goes George's wage. One less teacher.

The water dripping from the light causes the bulb to fizz and blow. The emergency workers come on and the rest of the performance will happen under them.

I'm really bored of you now.

SARAH: You're not going to discuss *this?*

TOM: I'm not going to discuss this with someone who has nothing new or intelligent to say, no.

SARAH: Fuck off!

SARAH: We should clear up this mess.

GEORGE: It can wait.

SARAH: No, it can't.

TOM: Oh here we go...

GEORGE moves over to help SARAH clear up.

LAURA: Sarah, you'll always be the same: hot air. All this talking yet *you* fuck up.

SARAH: ...

LAURA waits for SARAH to throw the glass into her face, she doesn't. Stalemate. LAURA decides to do it to herself.

The oil has reached the cables and plugs downstage. Everything cuts out. They wait, expecting to be stopped. Surely now a stage manager will come on? Someone will announce that this has to stop?

TOM: The end is here. Let's go.

This time, the box that contains Arthur hasn't been placed on the floor. TOM takes the box, in full view of the audience and the other actors, and places it on the floor. He stamps on it, all of his frustration released in that moment. TOM straightens out the box and place it back on the sofa. Uncertainty.

LAURA: This. Us. Everything. Is over.

SARAH: Finally!

TOM picks up the decanter and makes to leave.

SARAH: –

TOM: You can't take a gift. But...

SARAH just watches TOM. He eventually drops it.

It smashes.

TOM and LAURA attempt to exit. They slip, slide. It takes a lot longer than it should.

SARAH is staring at the mess. Everything holds different meaning for her now. The lines that belonged to SARAH totally belong in the actor's mouth now. The lines have blurred. GEORGE tries valiantly to keep the scene going but his concern for SARAH is beginning to show through. He's more concerned for her than the mess onstage.

E2.

GEORGE: There's no turning back now.

SARAH: End of something beautiful. Not that it was ever beautiful.

GEORGE: I've never seen anything like it.

SARAH: Can we just start again?

GEORGE: It's a bit late for that now. I wish we'd talked about all this sooner.

SARAH: Well, it was a bit difficult, wasn't it?

GEORGE: Are you feeling better?

SARAH: I can only see wrong choices. Things that will make everything worse. Ways to fuck up our already fucked up world.

GEORGE: Sarah, there is something beautiful about not letting things in.

SARAH: But it's everywhere. There's no way of not knowing anymore.

GEORGE: Because what difference does it make, really? If I worry about things I can't change? Start picking holes, all you'll see is darkness.

They stare at the oil. GEORGE goes and picks up Arthur.

Arthur will wake up. Like he has every year for the past twenty. And he will keep doing that every year for another fifty years?

SARAH is baffled, she thought they were on the same wave length, but the actor playing GEORGE is still carrying on with the performance. GEORGE puts Arthur down on the table.

GEORGE: What do you want to do with this? Ignore it? Yep, ignore it.

She goes and tops up her wine. Thick black oil.

They wait. Is it the end? Music comes somehow, tinny, from another speaker somewhere. Maybe TOM or LAURA are even playing it on their phone, desperate to keep the action going. SARAH watches on horrified as they reset to start everything again...

A3.

GEORGE and SARAH's living room. East London. The walls are no more. It is in chaos. GEORGE is dressing the table, the final preparations for a dinner party.

No lights except the emergency workers. No sound.

GEORGE tries desperately to ignore the mess, SARAH is fully in it, totally aware of it. Slowly, GEORGE can no longer maintain the Myth.

SARAH: It's complete fucking chaos...

GEORGE: What happened?

SARAH: Are you even listening to me? This is a massive fucking crisis. There's just too many people.

GEORGE: Calm down.

SARAH: I will not calm down!! It's so hot. It's meant to be bloody winter.

GEORGE: Which is why I'm so worried about –

SARAH: Oh for fuck's sake stop pretending!! How many more times do we have to do this before you acknowledge what's happening. They trod on him. He's dead!! Except he's not because it's just an empty box. So just stop it. Stop this.

GEORGE: *Sarah*, stop being so negative.

SARAH: You think you're being a nice guy but actually all you're doing is enabling the end of civilization.

GEORGE: It's going to be okay. Just calm down.

SARAH: We need to talk about/

GEORGE: Did you get the wine?

SARAH: / this. We need to stop this now.

GEORGE: You're making this sound less positive than I imagined.

SARAH: This is my worst nightmare. What on earth were we thinking? How have we even created this mess? We need to stop this right now.

GEORGE: It's too late.

SARAH: It's never too late.

GEORGE: Actually, this time it is.

SARAH: I didn't think this is where we'd end up.

GEORGE: I know. But isn't that amazing, we're on a true adventure, not knowing what the future has in store.

SARAH: We've run out of time –

Everything has fallen apart. TOM and LAURA, on hearing the line that is normally given to them on their entrance, attempt to join the scene. Not that scenes exist anymore. An awkward moment. TOM has no decanter as they have all smashed.

TOM: This place is just gorgeous.

GEORGE: Just ignore the chaos.

SARAH: We ran out of time –

LAURA: It looks fantastic. It's such a bold statement.

TOM: Very canny investment.

LAURA: And so, what next?

GEORGE: You put the gnocchi in here, and it griddles it for you.

SARAH: We've made a horrible mistake.

TOM: Who swiped right first?

SARAH: No, no sorry, we need to stop now. Can somebody?

GEORGE: Actually now's probably not the right time. Let's talk about it later?

LAURA: Clock is ticking. I know so many people who have left it too late.

SARAH: We've not talked about it.

LAURA: Doing nothing is making a decision.

GEORGE: We can carry on as we are or change everything.

SARAH: We need to change everything. Can we just start again please?

GEORGE: It's a bit late for that now.

LAURA: It's fine.

SARAH: Clearly everything is not fine.

LAURA: This whole situation will make you look at the future in a different light.

TOM: Laura –

LAURA: I'm trying to help.

TOM: I know, but perhaps tread carefully –

LAURA: I fought my natural instincts for so long…

They all look to SARAH. She's totally overwhelmed by the state of the stage: the oil, the water, the rubbish and the disintegration of their carefully constructed set.

SARAH: I'm sorry, I think we should stop. Can we stop? Please? Can someone please just do something about this?

LAURA: To listen to you you'd think the world is ending.

SARAH: It is.

TOM: She's always having a crisis. But it won't actually change anything.

SARAH: This isn't a joke.

The world of the play has now collapsed beyond salvation. All of the performers are now aware of this.

GEORGE: There's no turning back now.

SARAH: No, that's not true.

TOM: There's no turning back now.

LAURA: This. Us. Everything. Is over.

SARAH: I wish we'd talked about all this sooner.

GEORGE: I had never seen anything like it.

SARAH: End of something beautiful.

GEORGE: There is something beautiful about not letting things in.

SARAH: It's everywhere. There's no way of not anymore.

GEORGE: So…what are we going to do with this?

They look to SARAH for an answer.

SARAH: We clean up this mess.

Blackout.